ISBN 978-0-366-79145-3
PIBN 11352544

Forgotten Books is a registered trademark of FB &c Ltd.
Copyright © 2018 FB &c Ltd.
FB &c Ltd, Dalton House, 60 Windsor Avenue, London, SW19 2RR.
Company number 08720141. Registered in England and Wales.

For support please visit www.forgottenbooks.com

1 MONTH OF
FREE
READING

at

www.ForgottenBooks.com

By purchasing this book you are eligible for one month membership to ForgottenBooks.com, giving you unlimited access to our entire collection of over 1,000,000 titles via our web site and mobile apps.

To claim your free month visit:
www.forgottenbooks.com/free1352544

English
Français
Deutsche
Italiano
Español
Português

www.forgottenbooks.com

Mythology Photography **Fiction**
Fishing Christianity **Art** Cooking
Essays Buddhism Freemasonry
Medicine **Biology** Music **Ancient
Egypt** Evolution Carpentry Physics
Dance Geology **Mathematics** Fitness
Shakespeare **Folklore** Yoga Marketing
Confidence Immortality Biographies
Poetry **Psychology** Witchcraft
Electronics Chemistry History **Law**
Accounting **Philosophy** Anthropology
Alchemy Drama Quantum Mechanics
Atheism Sexual Health **Ancient History**
Entrepreneurship Languages Sport
Paleontology Needlework Islam
Metaphysics Investment Archaeology
Parenting Statistics Criminology
Motivational

DISSERTATIONS

ON THE

RHETORIC, PROSODY AND RHYME

OF

THE PERSIANS.

———◆———

By FRANCIS GLADWIN, Esquire.

Calcutta, printed:

Reprinted, in London, at the ORIENTAL PRESS, *by Wilson & Co.*

FOR J. DEBRETT, OPPOSITE BURLINGTON HOUSE, PICCADILLY.

———

1801.

ADVERTISEMENT.

———

THE following pages are extracted and compiled from the Muj-má us Su-ny-eh *of* Nizám eddeen Ahmed, *the* Arooz *of* Syfee, *and the* Cá-fe-yeh *of* Shums-ed-deen, *works of distinguished merit in the Persian Language; although the style is in many places somewhat obscure and perplexed, and the rules in general too prolix and diffuse.—To remedy these inconveniences, by combining perspicuity with conciseness, is the present intention, in order to render the Publication more useful and agreeable to the English Reader.*

PART I.

COMPOSITION.

PART I.

COMPOSITION.

Of the different Kinds of Composition.

Elm bu-de-a علم بديع is the art of arranging the words of a discourse with elegance and precision.

A composition is either in prose or in verse. Prose is of three kinds: 1. *Meh-ruj-juz* مرجز, or poetical prose, háving measure without rhyme: 2. *Meh-suj-jeh* مسجع, having rhyme without any measure: 3. *Aa-ree* عاري, simple prose, devoid both of rhyme and of measure. Neither rhyme without measure, nor measure without rhyme, is poetry; it being necessary that both should be combined to form verse.

Poetical composition is of ten kinds: 1. *Ghuz-el* غزل; 2. *Ka-see-deh* قصيده; 3. *Tush-beeb* تشبيب; 4. *Ke-tá-a* قطعه; 5. *Ru-bá-ee* رباعي; 6. *Fird* فرد; 7 *Mus-ne-wee* مثنوي; 8. *Tir-jee-a* ترجيع; 9. *Mo-sum-mut* مسمط; 10. *Mos-ta-zád* مستزاد.

1. The word غزل *Ghuz-el* (or Ode) literally signifies taking delight in the conversation of the fair sex, and is used technically for several couplets composed in one measure. The first couplet is called *Mo-sur-reh* مصرع, being a pair of rhyming hemistichs, and which couplet is now more commonly called *Mutla* مطلع. It is a general rule, that the *Ghuzel* do not contain more than twelve distichs—although some Poets formerly made *Ghuzels* of greater length; but now the rule is never transgressed. The common subjects of a *Ghuzel* are, the beauty of a mistress, and the sufferings of a lover, and the praise of love and friendship, under various circumstances. Sometimes it may treat of other matters, such as the mystical doctrines of the Soofees, the commendation of wine or hilarity. It is addressed, either to a mistress, or some other person, as the topic may require. It is thought best for the Poet to conceal his name until the last couplet; although few paid regard to this rule before the time of Sady, since which period it has generally been observed.

2. The *Ka-see-deh* قصيده (or Idyllium) resembles the *Ghuzel*, excepting that the *Ka-see-deh* must consist of more than twelve distichs. The subject may be either praise or satire, morality, or other matters. It is usual, in the *Ka-see-deh*, to have two or three of the distichs composed of rhyming hemistichs, which is the same as *Mutla* already described; although, according to some, the description of *Mutla* is confined to the first distich: but, in all cases when the Poet wishes to introduce into the *Ka-see-deh* a second *Mutla*, it is proper for him to intimate his intention in the preceding line. The

Du-á-tá-beed دعاي تابيد, signifying, "as long as such a thing endures, may you exist!" is proper at the conclusion of a *Ka-see-deh*, whose subject is praise. With the Arabians the *Ka-see-deh* hath no determinate number of lines, insomuch that they sometimes make it exceed five hundred distichs. The most eminent amongst the Persians have fixed the greatest extent of the *Ka-see-deh* at one hundred and twenty distichs.

3. *Tush-beeb* تشبيب signifies a representation of the season of youth and beauty, being a description of one's own feelings in love; but, in common use, it implies that praise which is bestowed on any thing, and the relation of circumstances, whether in celebration of love, or any other subject. The distichs, from the commencement of the *Ka-see-deh*, until the eulogium or *Me-dah* مدح, including every thing that the Poet wishes to describe, and which they call *Tush-beeb*, is a species of *Ghuzel*. But, in the *Ka-see-deh*, it is necessary that the descriptive distichs be followed by a *Te-khu-lus* تخلص, which is a transition from the description to the eulogium in a proper manner. A *Ka-see-deh* not having such a transition, is called *Muk-te-zeb* مقتضب; and when it is devoid of description, being an eulogium from the beginning to end, it is named *Mo-jud-dud* مجدد.

4. *Ke-tá-a* قطعه literally signifies a payment of any thing; but in poetry it means some distichs corresponding in measure and rhyme, but without a *Mutla*.

5. *Ru-bá-ee* رباعي (tetrastich) consists of two distichs corresponding in cadence, and composed in a measure peculiar to itself: but for the third hemistich, it is not necessary that it should rhyme with the fourth; however there is no rule to the contrary.

6. *Fird* فرد is a single distich, or *Biet* بيت, whose hemistichs may rhyme or not as the Poet pleases.

7. *Mus-ne-wee* مثنوي is composed of distichs corresponding in measure, each consisting of a pair of rhymes; and besides which the distichs have distinct poetical endings. This species of poetry is also called *Mooz-de-wuj* مزدوج (or wedded).

The explanation of *Mo-sum-mut*, *Tir-jee-e*, and *Mos-ta-zád,* will be given in the proper place.

Of the Construction of Words.

To those skilled in the construction of language, it is well known that the rules which have been laid down for the management thereof, by men of skill and learning, are very numerous; but, in this humble attempt, the author has collected together such only as are of general use, and most worthy of consideration.

The art of *Tir-see-a* coming most properly under the head of *Mutla*, and being the most conspicuous part of a composition, I shall therefore commence with it.

Tir-see-a ترصيع is an Arabic word, signifying, setting jewels in any thing : and, in composition, is when the author, in prose or in verse, divides his sentence into distinct parts, and assigns to each word another corresponding with it in measure and in rhyme. As an example, I shall quote a distich from Ab-dul Wa-sa-e Je-be-lee.

آرا يش آفاق شد رخسار بزم آرا ي تو
آسايش عشاق شد ديدار روح افزاي تو

" Thy cheek, the ornament of the banquet, embellished the universe :
the lovers were comforted by thy soul-enlivening presence."

Tir-see-a má-ul Tuj-nees ترصيع مع التجنيس . *Tir-see-a*, in itself, is a great beauty; but when united with *Tuj-nees*, or re- semblance in the form of the words, the effect is greatly heightened. Thus:

من نياز ارم ار تو ناز اري
من نياز آرم ار تو ناز اري

" I shall not be distressed, if you do not distress me::
I shall be wishful, if you are sportive."

Tuj-nees تجنيس literally signifies similarity, and, in rhetoric, is when the author uses two or more words resembling each other in writing or in speech, but having different significations: and of these there are seven kinds: 1. *Tuj-nee-se tám* ; 2. *Tuj-nee-se ná-kus* ; 3. *Tuj-nee-se zá-yed*; 4. *Tuj-nee-se mo-ruck-kub* ; 5. *Tuj-nee-se mo-kur-rur*; 6. *Tuj-nee-se mo-tur-ruf*; 7. *Tuj-nee-se-khut.*

1. *Tuj-nee-se tám* تجنيس تام is when two words are the same in sound and in form, but have different significations, without any variation in the vowel points.

اثرر ويي ترانسبت بشكل كردم غلطا كردم
وكرموىي ترا مشك خطا كفتم خطا كفتم

" If I compared your cheek to the rose, I committed a mistake: and if I called your hair Musk of Tartary, I uttered an impropriety."

2. *Tuj-nee-se ná-kus* تجنيس ناقص is when the different significations depend solely upon the vowel points.

دوشينه كه برد برد برد وشم بود
زانوچوعروس نو در آغوشم بود
پوشيدنيم نبود غير از چشم
چيز يكه بزبر سر نهم كوشم بود

" Last night, when the sheet of frigidity was upon my back; my knees, like those of a new bride, were drawn up to my ears. I had no covering excepting for mine eyes: the only things which I could place under my head, were my ears."

The foregoing example is used for the sake of the first hemistich, wherein بُرد *Boord* signifies a sheet, and بَرد *Bird* is frigidity.

3. *Tuj-nee-se zá-yed* تجنیس زاید is when two words occur together, one of which has a letter more than the other, as یار and دیار ,, . . خانه and خان — کنار and کار — دیار

4. *Tuj-nee-se mo-ruk-kub* تجنیس مرکب is when two words of the same form occur together, one in its simple primitive state, and the other as a compound. Examples: تابنده *Tá-bun-deh*, or *as long as the servant*, and تابنده *Ta-bin-deh*, or *shining*; نیازارد *Ne-yá-za-rud*, or *hurt him not*, and نیازارد *Ne-yaz-a-rud*, or *he will supplicate*; ترسابي *Tir-sá-ee*, or *an infidel*, and بي‌ترس‌ايي *Bey-tirs-á-ee*, or *come without fear*; لب‌ترسابي *Lub-e tir-sa-ee*, or *wipe the moist lip*.

5. *Tuj-nee-se mo-kur-rur* تجنیس مکرر is when, at the close of a period or verse, two words of the same form occur immediately one after the other.

اشکر چه هست شکلت را چومن هزار هزار

" Although you have given others, as well as myself, a thousand thousand (or a thousand nightingales)."

In such case, it is allowable to prefix an additional letter to either of the words; for example, کنار and تلر — مکار and کار.

It may happen, that, for the sake of the measure, an extraneous word or letter is introduced. Thus:

اتنا د مرا بادل مكار تو كار

" It so happened that I had a concern with your deceitful heart."

6. *Tuj-nee-se mo-tur-ruf* تجنيس مطرف is when two words are used, differing only in the final letter, such as شراب and شرار — افات and افاق .

7. *Tuj-nee-se khut* تجنيس خط is when the linear forms of words are the same, the different significations depending upon either the diacritical or the vowel points, or on both, as مسكين *Miskeen,* or *poor,* and مشكين *Mooshkeen,* or *musky,* بخل *Parsimony,* نخل *a date tree,* نحل *a bee.*

Ish-te-kak اشتقاق literally signifies to split, and, in the language of Rhetoricians, is when words are brought together whose letters approximate in sound ; and it is desirable that they should be derived from the same primitive. Some of the most elegant Persian writers do not consider this as a separate art, but reckon it only a species of *Tujnees.*

گر ذره ز مهر قبولت بهن رسد
درثروت از ثري به ثريا برد مرا

" If an atom of the sun of your approbation is imparted unto me, its riches will elevate me from the earth to the pleiades."

Suj-á سجع literally signifies the cooing of doves, and is used technically, in three ways. 1. *Suj-á-e mo-te-wá-zee* سجع متوازي when at the end of two periods of prose, or at the close of two hemistichs in verse, there are used two words agreeing in measure, in rhyme, and in the final letter, and the number of letters in each being equal.

گلشن امروز عجب تازه بهاري دارد
بلبل وكل بچمن قول و تراري دارد

" The flower garden to-day hath a wonderful freshness of spring:
the nightingale and the rose form their engagements in the
flower bed."

Here the words بهاري and تراري are *Suj-á* or responsive.

2. *Suj-á mo-tur-ruf* سجع مطرف is when two hemistichs, or in two periods of prose, some words correspond with others in the final letter, but differ in measure, as well as in the number of the letters, such as اطوار and وقار — خال and خيال .

3. *Suj-á mo-wá-ze-neh* سجع موازنه is when, throughout two hemistichs, words are used that correspond in measure, but differ in the final letters.

ریشک نظم من خورد حسان ثابت راجكر
دست نثر من زند سحبان وایل را تغا

c

" The envy of my verses devours the liver of Hussan Sabit: the
arm of my prose smiteth the neck of Seh-ban-é Wa-yel."*

Muck-loob مقلوب (or anagram) literally signifies inverted, and
tehnically is when a change is made in order of some or of all the
words composing a sentence. The most common species are the
four following : 1. *Muck-loob-é báz* مقلوب بعض when in a sentence, the order of some of the letters are transposed, thus : رشك
transposed into شكر, and جاد وانه into جاود انه

2. *Muck-loob-é kool* مقلوب كل, when some words in a sentence are anagrams of one another, thus :

راي تو يار صواب داد تو محض وداد
فتح توحتنف حسود ضيف تو فيض مراد

" † Your wisdom is a meritorious friend, your justice is friendship
     in extreme ; your victory is the death of the envious man, your
     being host gratifies desire."

3. *Muck-loob-e Mo-je-neh* مقلوب مجنح is when, in the same
distich or hemistich, words occur at the beginning and at the end,
which are anagrams of each other.

---

* Two rival authors.

† In the translation nothing more can be attempted than giving the sense of the words.
The anagrams are فيض and ضيف—حتنف and فتح—يار and راي

رام شد دل بآن بت طرار
لبش افسون گراستوز لغش مار

" The heart is obedient to that deceitful idol ; her lips are enchan-
ters, and her locks are snakes."

4. *Muck-loob-e Moos-te-wee* مقلوب مستوي is when a sentence may be read forwards and backwards, with one signification ;
and that is the most difficult species of anagram.

ارا م داد داد ما را .آرام .— He gave me rest.

Rud-dool uj-ze a-luss sud-re رد العجز علي الصدر . *Ujz*
properly signifies the last, and *Sudr* the first word of a hemistich:
but here the sense is not so restricted; this art consisting in using
the same word in any two parts of the distich, and which may be
done in six ways.

1: When the same word both begins and ends the distich :

شيدا شده ام چرا همي نهي
زنجير دو زلف بر من شيدا

" Since I am become a madman—why cast you not the chain of
those two locks upon me, a madman ?"

يگانه زمانه شدستي وليكن
نشد هيچکس را زمانه يگانه

" You had been the unique of the age; but that time hath been no
one's friend."

In this example, the word يِگانه signifies " unique," and also " a
friend."

2. When the word used in the middle of the first hemistich, also
concludes the distich:

ما را که کند مسلم انجا که

خورشید نهي شون مسلم

" Who will consider us perfect in that place, where the sun is not
(deemed) perfect ?"

يوسف ماست ببا زاز کنون جلوه فروش

زاهد ازگوشه خلوت دل خود را بازار

" Our Joseph, in the market-place of Canaan, displays his worth:
O hermit, bring back your heart to the cell of retirement !"

Here the word بازار signifies " market-place," and also " bring
back."

3. When the words so used are derived from the same verb, but
have different inflections :—

بکوشش گشت قدر هر یگي در پیش یار افزون

من مسکین زبون تر مي شوم هر چند میکوشم

" By exertion in the presence of his mistress, every one increases his value; but I, hapless wretch! am worse the more I exert myself."

4. When two words are used that somewhat resemble each other, but are of different derivations and significations:

نارد از خدمت تو بیرون سر

گرچه بشکافیش به نیزه چونار

" He will not quit your service, although you were to split his head with a spear, as you would serve a pomegranate."

5. When the same word concludes both hemistichs:

ای ساربان آهسته ران کارام جانم میرود

آن دل که باخود داشتم بادل ستانم میرود

" O camel-driver, proceed slowly, seeing that the comfort of my life is departing; that heart which I had kept for myself, accompanies the mistress of my affections."

6. When the last hemistich begins and ends with the same word:

نه در دشت سبزی نه در باغ شخ

ملخ بوستان خورد و مردم ملخ

" Neither was there on the plain any verdure, nor in the garden a branch: the locusts devoured the garden, and the men devoured the locusts."

Ay-nát اعنات is when the author labours to effect a point that is not necessary, the sense being complete without it: For example, when, at the end of a cadence or rhyme, he foists in a letter before the final letter, or before the *Ridf* ردف, which is the quiescent before the last letter of the rhyme. Thus, ق in the words رفم and بقم ; whereas رقم might rhyme with علم: However, uniformity is certainly an ornament. This art is called *Il-te-zám wul lú-zoome má-lá yel-zum* التزام ولزوم مالا يلزم .

Example.

اي نكو خواه دولت توعزيز
اي بد انديش روزگار توخوار
هركه زنهارخواه عهد توكشت
مسپارش بعالم خونخوار

" He who wisheth you prosperity, is esteemed; he who wisheth
you evil, is despised. Whosoever seeketh refuge in your time,
deliver him not up to the blood-thirsty world."

In this example, if the rhyme to خوار had been نار, it would
also have been correct.

Lu-zoom لزوم is when the Poet imposes any task upon himself,
such as when Syfee of Nishapoor resolved to introduce the words
سيم and سنگ into every hemistich of a *Ká-see-deh*, of which the
following lines are a specimen :

اي نگار سنگ دل وي لعبت سيمين عذ ار
مهر نو اندر دلم چون سيم در سنگ استوار

" O flinty-hearted mistress, a puppet with silver cheeks; my affection for you is fast fixed in my heart, like silver in the
ore."

Another Example from Catebi.

مرا غمی است شتر بارها به حجرهٔ تن

شتر دلی نکنم غم کجا و حجرهٔ من

" I have camel-loads of cares in the chamber of my body: I am not
camel-hearted; where then will care find a place in my body?"

Tuz-meen ul-mooz-de-wuj تضمين المزدوج is when the author,
in verse or in prose, after forming the cadence and the rhyme, introduces two or more words which are termed *Mooz-de-wuj*, corresponding in final letter with the rhyme, thus:

دور از رخ فرخ مه مهر گسل

شد نورو سرور دو راز دیده و دل

رخ زر دو بسینه درد و در جان آتش

من زار چنین یار ز حالم غافل

" Separated from the happy countenance of my inconstant mistress,
light and gladness were removed from my eyes and heart; the
cheek pallid, the breast oppressed with pain, and the soul on
fire. I am in this woful plight, whilst she is regardless of my
condition."

Moo-te lu-vun متلون or various, is when the Poet composes

a distich which may be read in two or more measures, by a little variation of the accent, thus:

اي شده در خانه جان منزلت
خانه جان يافته زان منزلت

" Yes, you have taken up your residence in the mansion of my
    soul: the mansion of my soul hath obtained dignity thereby."

This distich may be read in the measure of محذوف رمل مسدس
and also of سريع مطوي مكشوف

There is another species of *Moo-te loo-vun*, when, upon some words being rejected, the distich assumes another measure, without injuring the sense. For example, in the two following distichs, the words which are scored may be struck out, when the measure will be changed, but the sense continue the same.

نصرة الد ين اي جهان بخشي كه از اقبال هست ·
تيغ عالمگير تو روز ظفر مالك رقاب
برده در شگاه و عكس نور راي رو شنت
پرده صبح سحر خيز است و نور آ فتاب

" Nuss-rut-ed-deen, thou who art the bestower of life, (through your
    auspices.) Your sword, the conqueror of the world (in the
    day of victory), is the sovereign of necks. The veil of thy pa-
    lace and (the reflected splendour of) thy enlightened mind, are
    the curtain of the (early) dawn, and the light of the sun."

Zoo-ká-fe-ye-tyn ذوقافيتين is when the Poet places two rhymes close together, thus :

اي از مكارم تو شده در جهان خبر

انگنده از سياست تو آسمان سپر

" Yes, the fame of your benevolence is spread throughout the
world ; your government disarms the sky."

And if he uses more than two such rhymes in a distich, it is
termed *Zool-ke-wa-fee* ذوالقوافي , thus :

گر سعد شود طالع و اختر يارت

دارا شودت تابع و پر زر دارت

" If the star of your nativity is your friend, Darius may obey you,
and your house be filled with gold."

Mo-wush sheh موشح (or the acrostic). This word is derived
from توشيح, which literally signifies, putting round the neck a
collar inlaid with precious stones : but here it means, when the Poet
makes such arrangement of his verses, that the initials of each line,
being put together, form some word or verse.

ما كه ميشكوء بيم توحيد خدا

باد متقبول جناب كبريا

احمد و اصحاب و آلش رامدام

رحمت حق باد از ما و السلام

كرده شد اين نسخه تاريخ ونام

جمله در ابواب منظومه تمام

The initials of the above lines are an acrostic of the Poet's name
مبارک ; and the numerical value of the letters, forming the title of
the book, give the date when it was written, viz. A. H. 1053, or
A. D. 1643.   It is impossible to render the lines into English in the
form of an acrostic; but the following is a literal translation:

" I declare the Unity of God; may it be acceptable at the Divine
    threshold ! Ahmed and his companions and family for ever!
    May the mercy of God, I pray, be upon them, and peace!
    The title of this book expresses also the date when it was
    written."

Mo-suj-ja مسجع is when the Poet divides a distich into four
equal parts, and, after preserving the same rhyme for three of them,
makes the fourth in the rhyme which is the burden of the poem.

من ما نده ام مهجور از و دلخسته و رنجور ازو
گویی که نیشی دوز ازو در استخوانم میر ود
باز آی و در چشم نشین ای دلستان نازنین
کاشوب و فریاد از زمین تا آسمانم میر ود

" Smitten with heart-felt woe, I have remained separated from her;
    you might say, in her absence a sting invades my bones. Re-
    turn, and set yourself in my eyes, O charming ravisher of my
    heart ! for my lamentations and cries reach from earth to
    heaven."

Huzf (حذف) is when the Author labours to prevent the introduction of some particular letter or letters, like Sulmán, who has composed an elegy, throughout which the letter Alif never occurs.

The two most ingenious kinds of *Huzf* are *Ta-teel* تعطيل and *Mun-koot* منقوط. The first is when the Author rejects all letters that have diacritical points. The book intitled *Se-wa-ta-ul il-ham* سواطع الالهام, a commentary on the Koran by Sheikh Fizee, the brother of Abulfázel, is written in conformity to this rule, from beginning to end, without a single letter that has a diacritical point. On the contrary, *Munkoot* is a composition, in which all the letters have diacritical points. The last kind is more difficult than the other. Ameer Khusro, in the Ai-jaz Khusro-wee, (اعجاز خسروي) has several excellent letters written in both these ways.

Mo-rud-duf (مردف) is when the Poet composes in the *Redeef* form. *Re-deef* رديف is the reiteration of one or several words after the rhyme is complete. The *Morud-duf* form is very usual in Persian poetry, but has never been used by any good Arabian Poet. The following example is from Jami:

دو چشم يار که مستند و ناتوان هر دو
شدند آفت عقل و بلاي جان هر دو
ميان ما و تو جزجان و تن حجاب نبود
بيا که هجر تو برد اشت از ميان هر دو

" The two eyes of my mistress, which are wanton and languishing, ' both of them ;' overpower wisdom, and destroy life, ' both of them.' Between you and I, excepting soul and body, there

is no partition. Come, since your absence hath severed soul
and body, ' both of them—' "

Some, instead of *Re-deef*, call it *Há-jib* حاجب, and *Morud-duf*
verse they term *Meh-joob* محجوب. But, according to some, *Hajib*
is the word immediately preceding the rhyme of a distich, as in the
following verses the word داري precedes the rhymes تخت and
سخت and لخت and بخت

اي شاه زمين بر آسمان داري تخت

سست است عدو تاتو كهان داري سخت

حمله سبك آري و گران داري لخت

پيري تو بد انش وجوان داري بخت

" O king of the earth! your throne is seated in heaven: weak is your
enemy, since you have a strong bow: you make a slight at-
tack, and commit great havock: you are old in wisdom, whilst
your fortune enjoys the vigour of youth."

Re-deef رديف in the common acceptation of the word, is a
person riding behind another on the same horse.

Te-rá-fuc ترافق are verses composed in such a manner that any
two hemistichs thereof may be taken indifferently, and yet form a
complete distich, without the Poem suffering injury either in signification, in rhyme, or in measure.

ازز لف برون کني اکرتاب شوم
بر لب ننهي اکر مي ناب شوم
درچشم نیا وري اکر خواب شوم
از دست فرو ریزي اکر آب شوم

" Reject me from your locks, if I be a ringlet; suffer me not to touch your lips, if I be pure wine; bring me not to your eyes, if I be sleep; pour me from your hands, if I be water."

Mo-sum-mut مسمط is when the Poet composes some hemistichs of the same measure and rhyme, and closes the last hemistich with the prevailing rhyme of the Poem.

Examples of Triplets.

عا شقیم و شعار ما اینست
اینچنینیم و کار ما اینست
شرف روز کار ما اینست

" I am a lover, and this is my custom; I am of such sort, and my occupation is this; the boast of my time is this."

سالها شد که زار و محر و نیم
بارخ زرد و اشک کلکونیم
که خزان و بهار ما اینست

" For years past, I have been afflicted and distressed with pallid cheeks and rose-coloured tears; for such is my autumn and my spring."

هردم از دوري رخ ماهي
ميكشم از دل حزين آهي
شمع شبهاي تار ما اينست

" Every moment that I am absent from the cheek of my mistress, I
utter a sigh from my afflicted heart: this is the candle of my
dark night."

آنكه چون روي او گلي نشگفت
حيرتي را چو ديد خندان گفت
عاشق خاكسار ما اينست

" Her, whose cheek the bloom of the rose cannot equal; when she
beheld Hi-ruttee, said, laughingly, This is my humble lover."

Example of Tretrasticks.

زامدن نوبهار باغ چو بت خانه شد
گشت رخ گل چو شمع باد چوپروانه شد
پيشه بلبل كنون گفتن افسانه شد
گل زخوشي پاره كرد برتن خود پيرهن

" From the arrival of spring, the garden resembles an idol temple;
the cheek of the rose represents the candle; and the wind may
be compared to the moth; the business of the nightingale is
now to relate tales; the rose bursts the vestments of its body
through joy."

Example of Pentasticks.

در عشق تو اي صنم چنا نم
كز هستي خويش در كها نم
هر چند كه زار و نا توانم
گر دست دهد هزار جا نم
در پاي مباركت فشا نم

" Such is my affection for thee, idol of my soul ! that I even doubt
my own existence : however I may be distressed and weak,
if you bestow your hand, I possess a thousand lives, which I
would devote at your happy feet."

Example of Hexasticks.

اي عشق تو با جان من از مبداء فطرت
وصل تو صفاي دل و هجر تو كدورت
صورت نتوان بست كه از خامه قدرت
پيدا شده باشد چو رخ خوب تو صورت
ني كسوت ادراك تو بر قامت فكرت
ني دامن او صاف تو در دست فصاحت

" Yes, the affection which I have for you in my soul, was formed
from the first interview. Your presence purifies the heart, and
your absence disturbs it. The imagination cannot conceive
how the pen of fate could create a countenance so beautiful as
thine : imagination cannot conceive your perfections ; neither
can eloquence reach the skirt of your excellencies."

Another of Hexasticks.

بیرون ز وصال تو دلم را طلبی نیست
جز یاد تو در خاطر غمگین طربی نیست
در کشور خربی چو تو یاقوت لبی نیست
تاریکتر از روز فراق تو شبی نیست
فریاد من سوخته دل بی سببی نیست
دود از سر آتش رود و خون زجراحت

" Besides the desire of your compauy, my heart hath no wish:
besides the contemplation of yourself, my sorrowful heart hath
no enjoyment. In the region of beauty, there are no ruby
lips to be compared to thine. No night is darker than the day
when you are absent. The complaint of my burning heart
is not without cause: smoke issues from flame, and blood
from a wound."

Mos-ta-zád, مستزاد is when a line of Prose is introduced after a
hemistich or a distich, the sense of which prose line must be connected with the poetry, but the verse must be so constructed as to
be complete without it:

فارغ ز شراب صاف گلرنگ مباش
چون درد کشان
بی باده و مطرب خوش آهنگ مباش
در دیر مغان

چون لاله قدح گیر و چو گل خندان شو
در گلشن دهر
یعني که بسان غنچه دلتنگ مباش
در باغ جهان

" Quit not the pure and rosy wine,

        Like dreg-drinkers :

Be not without wine and melodious minstrels,

        In the house of the vintners :

Take the cup resembling the tulip, and smile thou like the rose,

        In the garden of time ;

That is, let not your heart be contracted like a rose-bud,

        In the garden of the world."

Another Example.

رفتم بطبیب و گفتمش بیمارم
از اول شب تا بسحر بیدارم
در مانم چیست
نبضم چو طبیب دید گفت از سر لطف
جز عشق نداري مرضي پندارم
محبوب تو کیست

" I went to the physician, and said to him, I am sick,

 . I lie awake from night until morning ;

        What is my remedy ?

When the physician felt my pulse, he kindly said,

I think you have no disorder but love;

> Who is your mistress ?"

Another Example.

رفتم بر يار و گفتمش دلد ارم

داغي زغم عشق تو بر دل دارم

درمن نظر يست

گفتا تو کدام درد مندي چه کسي

صد عاشق چون تو در سلا سل دارم

گو نام تو چيست

" I went to my beloved, and said to her, O my heart !

I carry in my breast a wound caused by the grief of love.

> She stared at me.

She asked, who and what art thou, who thus complain ?

I hold a hundred such lovers in my chains.

> Say what is your name ?"

Ukhs عکس (Inversion)¡ is when the same words which commence a sentence are reversed to conclude it. This form is also called *Tub-deel* تبديل or interchange.

در چهرهٔ تو ديدم لطفي که مي شنيدم

لطفي که مي شنيدم در چهرهٔ تو ديدم

" In your countenance I beheld that beauty of which I had heard.
That beauty of which I had heard, in your countenance I beheld."

Amongst the variety of *Ukhs,* is when the same words are read
both backwards and forwards, in the manner of the anagram,
excepting that there letters, and here whole words, are transposed.

در مي داري و داري كرمي

كرمي دازي و داري درمي

" You possess money, and you possess liberality: liberality you
possess, and money you possess."

با حسان توبي حاتم برفعت توبى كسري

بغرمان توبى آصف به برهان توبي عيسي

" In liberality you are Hatem, in dignity you are Cæsar; in command you are Asof, in argument you are Jesus."

Reversed.

عيسي توبي به برهان آصف توبي بغرمان

كسري توبي برفعت حاتم توبي با حسان

" You are Jesus in argument, you are Asof in. command; you are
Cæsar in dignity, you are Hatem in liberality."

Mo-kur-ur مكرر, or reiteration, is when a word is repeated in
the same distich as hemistich.

روي تو صفحه صفحه و هر صفحه افتاب

موي تو حلقه حلقه و هر حلقه ز وطناب

زان صفحه صفحه صفحه ٔ كل شد ورق ورق

زان حلقه حلقه حلقه ٔ سنبل به پيچ و تاب

" Your cheeks resemble two leaves, and each leaf is the sun. Your hair hangs in ringlets, and each ringlet is a cord (*to bind your lovers*). From envy of those leaves, the leaves of the rose are expanded. From envy of those ringlets, the spike-nard becomes twisted."

Ruk-ta رتنا is the name of a species of sheep of a grey colour; and this term is used by Rhetoricians, for a species of composition wherein the letters are with and without diacritical points alternately.

خدنگ غمزه شوخ مغ صنوبر قد

زكند شست هنر خسته جان مير جليل

Khy-fú خيفا is a horse, one of whose eyes is black, and the other blue; and this term is applied to a composition wherein the words are with and without diacritical points alternately.

علم بينش دهد ببين دلرا

روح جنبش دهد ببين گلرا

Tus-gheer تصغير is the letter ك added at the end of a word when it is called *Kaf-tusgheer* كاف تصغير or the diminutive *Kaf*.

Sometimes it is used to express kindness and affection ; but generally to denote contempt, as in the following lines :

بتكي پياله بركف رخكش زباده كلثون
دلكم ربوده يكدم بد و لعلك پر افسون

" A little idol with a glass in her hand, her little cheeks tinged with rosy wine.   My little heart was captivated in an instant, by two little rubies full of enchantment."

Mo-kutta منقطع, or disjoined, is when the Author uses words composed of letters written separately, without any joinings :

دارم آه زار در دوري يار
ذوق دل زان روي دارم ارزو

The sense of which is,

" I utter many sighs in her absence; my heart being entirely bent upon beholding that face."

Moo-sul موصل, or joined, is the reverse of *Mokutta*, all the letters being joined together.

كر تو جانان خريف ماباشي
هيچ غم نيست غير قلا شي

" If thou, my beloved, art my friend, there is nothing to dread but poverty."

Tir-je-á ترجیع, or involving, is the name given to a species of poem formed of distinct parts, each part consisting of an equal number of distichs, never less than five, nor more than eleven. The rhyme of each stanza is different, each has a distinct *mutla*; and at the end of each stanza is an extraneous distich, connected in sense with the stanza, although the stanza is complete in itself. When the same extraneous distich is added to every stanza, it is called *Tir-je-á-bund* (ترجیع بند); but if these final distichs are various, they are called *Tir-keeb-bund* (ترکیب بند).

Tir-jee-a-bund, from Hafiz.

اي سرو سمنبر گل اندام   از عارض تو خجل مه تام

بازآي که هجر جانگدازت   برد از دل من قرار و آرام

ماییم و غم فراق و جانی   تا خود بکجا رسد سرانجام

جز محنت و درد کو بیانیست   دور از تو نصیب ماز ایام

حالی چو نمیشود مهیا   کام دلم از تو اي دلارام

آن به که زصبر رخ نتابم

باشد که مراد دل بیابم

در سختي عشق گر بمیرم   من دل زغم تو بر نگیرم

پیوسته کمان ابرو انت   از غمزه هي زنند تیرم

نتوان بقلم نوشت شوقم   گر تیر فلک شود دبیرم

پیر غم عشقم ارچه طفلم   طفل ره عشقم ارچه پیرم

چون کرد زمانه ستمگار   دور از توبه بند غم اسیرم

آن به که زصبر رخ نتابم

باشد که مراد دل بیابم

" O silver-bosomed cypress, a form delicate as the rose, the beauty of whose charms surpasseth the moon in her brightest splendor! return, for your absence melts my soul, and deprives my heart of ease and rest. Here are my body and my soul lamenting your absence: under such circumstances, how is it possible for me to exist? You would say, that, excepting grief and pain, destiny had bereft me of every thing in your absence. Seeing that I cannot now obtain the desire of my heart from you, the comfort of my life,

" It is best not to turn away my face from patience; perhaps I may yet obtain my heart's desire."

" Were 1 sure of dying under the pangs of love; nevertheless, my heart should not cease to grieve for you. Thy eyebrow, like a bow, smiteth incessantly with the arrows of amorus glances. The pen could not describe my longing desire, even although Mercury were to be my secretary. I am old in the sufferings of love, although but an infant; an infant in the paths of love, yet old in years. Seeing that, during your absence, tyrannic fortune holds me in the fetters of sorrow,

" It is best not to turn away my face from patience; perhaps I may yet obtain my heart's desire."

Mo-lum-ma ﻊﻠﻣ is when the Poet composes his hemistichs or

6

distichs in Persian and Arabic alternately, and which is allowable
as far as ten distichs in each language.

$$احن شو قاالي ديار لقيب فيها جمال سلبا$$
$$كه ميرساند ازان نواحي نويد لطغش بجانب ما$$

" I weep after the city where I had an interview with the beautiful
  Selima : who will bring me from that country the glad tidings
  of her kindness towards me ?"

Mo-se-huf مصحف is when words are used, which, upon the
changing the diacritical or the vowel-points, have meanings diametrically opposite. Thus the lines :

$$مادرت را هزار بوسه زدم$$
$$بدرت خود نبود الا من$$

may be read thus :

" I gave you a thousand kisses ; there was no one at your door
  excepting myself."

Or thus :

" I gave your mother a thousand kisses ; you had no father but
  myself."

Te-zul-zool تزلزل is when there is a word, of which, upon changing the vowel-point of one letter only, the sense is altered entirely.
Thus :

روزو شب خواهم همین از کرد ثار

تا سرت باشد همیشه تاجدار

" Day and night I am incessantly imploring God, that your head
may ever be crowned."

If the letter ج in تاجدار is made quiescent, *táj-dár*, it signifies
" crowned ;" but when it is accented, *tá-je-dar*, it means, " to, or
upon the wall."

Tuz-meen تضمین is when the Poet applies to his purpose some
lines from another author; but in case the author so quoted be not
well known, it is incumbent on him to mention the name, in order
to obviate the imputation of plagiarism.

Tá-reekh تاریخ (or date) is when, upon the occurrence of any
remarkable event, a word or a verse is made up of letters forming
the date thereof in the Hijera style. The beauty of this species of
composition consists in the words of the date being also applicable
to the circumstances of the event. Thus, when Sumbha, the Mah-
ratta chief, with his wife and children were taken prisoners by the
troops of Aurungzeeb, somebody expressed the date thereof in the
following hemistich :

بازن و فرزند سنبها شد اسیر

" Sumbha was made prisoner with his wife and children, or—
A. H. 1104."

Of Style and Sentiment.

Bud-e-ea má-no-wee بدايع معنوي or style and sentiment, on which the beauty of composition depends.

Ey-ham ايهام (or enigma), and which is also called *Tew-re-yut* تورية according to the Arabian rhetoricians, is when a sentence or a word is used with a doubtful meaning, so that the hearer may mistake the intention of the speaker; as in the following lines of Sady:

سعدي هزار جامه ز دستت قبا كند

يك مهر باني از تو بسالي نيافته

Mehr-bá-nee is the name of a kind of garment, and also signifies kindness; so that this distich may be taken in two senses:

" On your account Sady hath torn a thousand garments; whilst, in the course of a year, he hath not obtained of you one kindness, or one garment."

But the Persian Poets define *Ey-hám* to be using a word having several meanings, all equally applicable to the subject.

Example from Amed.

دل عكس رخ خوب تو در آب روان ديد

و اله شد و فرياد بر آورد كه ماهي

" My heart saw, in a running stream, the reflection of thy face;
enraptured, I exclaimed, Is it the moon!

The word *Máhee* has four meanings, equally applicable in this
place—1. the moon—2. water—3. a fish—4. what thing?

It is said, that Ameer Abool-burkát wrote and sent the following
distich to Meer Aly Sheir:

خشک شد کشت امید و قحط شد تخم و فا

زاتش غم تا در ابر چشم من یاران نباند

" The field of hope is parched up; there is a scarcity of the seed of
faithfulness. The fire of grief has totally exhausted the rain,
from the clouds of my eyes."

The diacritical points having been misplaced, or omitted, Meer-
Aly Sheir instead of تا read یا, and objected that the verse had no
meaning. When this was told to Abool-burkát, he sent the following verses:

هرچه آید به نزد اهل صواب

بکهان خطاش خط نکنند

هرچه خوانند نیک فکر کنند

یا بخوانند تا غلط نکنند

نقطها گرفتند بزیر و زبر

عقل را پیر و نقط نکنند

" Whatever cometh before men of upright intention, they do not
mark it with a line as faulty, merely upon conjecture of its being

erroneous : whatever they read, they well consider; or else they read it not, that they may not be mistaken. Admitting that the dots are misplaced, the sense does not depend upon dots."

Moh-te-me-looz zid-deen محتمل الضدين is when a sentence is introduced in such a manner that it will bear two constructions diametrically opposite to each other; such as praise, and satire. It is also called *Zoo-je-he-tain* ذوجهتين :

اي خواجه ضيا شود زروي توطلم
با طلعت تو سور نمايد ما تم

" Indeed, sir, your countenance converteth darkness into light : at your presence, mourning is changed into joy."

Or thus :

" Indeed, sir, light by your presence is turned into darkness : at your presence, joy is turned into sorrow."

There is a story, that a Sunnee and a Shee-ah being in a large company, asked a great personage, whom he esteemed to be the most excellent of mankind, next to the Prophet ? he answered,

من بنته في بيته

" That person whose daughter is in his house."

Which being applied to the daughter of Mohammed, is in favour of Aly; but, if applied to the daughter of Abubecre, gives the preference to him.

There is also a story of Akeel, that, being displeased with his brother Aly the Khalif, he went over to Moa-wi-yeh, who received him with great kindness and respect: but desired him to curse Aly; and, as he would not admit of any refusal, Akeel thus addressed the congregation:

ايها الناس اعلموا ان علي ابن ابي طالب اخي و امرنى
معاويه ان العنه فلعنت الله عليه

" O people! you know that Aly, the son of Aboo-tá-leb, is my
   brother; now Moa-wi-yeh hath ordered me to curse him, therefore may the curse of God be upon him!"

So that the curse would apply either to Aly or to Moa-wi-yeh.

Tush-beeh تشبيه (or simile) is to compare the quality of any thing to that of something else:

خشم تو قاهر چو نار و جود تو سايل چو آب
طبع تو صافي چو باد و حلم تو ثابت چو طين

" Your anger is violent, like fire; your liberality flows, like water;
   your mind is pure, like air; your clemency is immoveable, like
   the earth."

Tuf-seer تفسير or paraphrase, is when the Author writes first some subject summarily, and then enters into explanation and detail. Of *Tufseer* there are two species, 1. *Je-lee* جلي and 2. *Khe-fee* خفي

1. *Tufseer Jelee*, is when the Poet in an hemistich or distich uses words of doubtful meaning, requiring explanation; and therefore in another hemistich or distich, he explains the sense in repeating the same words :

يا به بندد يا كشايد يا ستاند يادهد

تا جهان بر پاي باشد شاه را اين باد كار

انچه بستاند و لايت و انچه بدهد خواسته

و انچه بندد پاي دشمن و انچه بكشايد حصار

" Either he will bind, or he will conquer; either he will take, or he will grant. As long as the world shall endure, may the king perform these exploits: take kingdoms, grant desires, bind the feet of his enemies, or conquer fortresses."

2. *Tufseer Khefee*, is when the Poet at first is concise and obscure, and then becomes diffusive and clear, but without repeating the words of the text in the commentary :

همي آرزد پيوسته زبهر جشن تو پيدا

همي زايند همواره زبهر بزم تو آسان

رطب نخل و عسل نحل و فريشم كرم و مشك آهو

درر در يا وزر خارا و شكر نال شكو هركان

" They produce incessantly for your delight ; they yield constantly
without labour, for your banquet ; the palm tree, fresh dates,
bees honey, worms silk, deer musk, the sea pearls, the stone
gold, the cane sugar, the mines precious stones."

Tákeed ul mu-deh bé ma-yesh bé hooz zum-mé تاكيد المدح
بهايشبه الذم is when the Author, celebrating a mistress, or some
great personage, after recounting their virtues in general, and wish-
ing to add other excellencies, proceeds with such a word that the
hearer may suspect he is going to satirize and expose faults ; so
that when he expatiates on their additional perfections, it excites
surprize :

عدل و انصاف تو شاها بكمال است و ليك
اينقدر هست كه در بدل نداري انصاف

" Your majesty's justice and equity are in perfection, excepting that
your liberality is so excessive that it hath no bounds."

Takeed uz zum-mé bé ma-yesh bé kul mu-deh تاكيد الذم
بهايشه المدح is the reverse of the foregoing :

ندارد خلق از و در همنه دينار
ولي دارند از و آزار بسيار

" Mankind partake not of his riches ; but they are obliged to him
for many injuries."

Hoos-nul tá-leel حسن التعليل or exaggeration, is when, in

4

order to extol any excellency, for the sake of a witticism, a comparison is used suitable thereto, but rather far fetched :

آن زلف خوشت که دل پسند افتاده است
از قد چو سروت چو کمند افتاده است
گفتم که چرا شکسته سر تا پایست
فرمود که از جاي بلند افتاده است

~ That delightful ringlet of thine, which charms the heart, has fallen like a noose from your cypress form. I asked, why is it thus twisted from head to foot ? It answered, because it has fallen from a lofty place."

So-wál ó jé-wáb سوال و جواب dialogue, called also *mo-rá-já-ut* مراجعت or return, is when the Poet asks a question, and answers it in the same hemistich, or makes one hemistich or one distich a question, and another the answer :

گفت جانان سوي من بگذر بسر گفتم بچشم
گفت ترك جان کن و درمن نگر گفتم بچشم

" My beloved said, come to me upon your head ; I answered, with my eyes, (i. e. I consent ;) she said, bid adieu to life, I replied, with my eyes."

گفتم سخنت شکسته وش چون آید
با انکه همه چو در مکنون آید
گفتاکه ازین دهان تنگی که مراست
تا نشکنمش چگونه بیرون آید

" I asked, Why are your words thus broken, whilst they all come forth like bright pearls ? She said, From this little mouth of mine, unless I break them, how can I utter them ?"

The dialogue is frequently carried on without saying, I asked, and she replied.

پیام دادم نزدیک آن بت کشمیر
که زیر حلقهٔ زلفت دلم چراست اسیر
جواب داد که دیوانه شد دل توز عشق
بره نیارد دیوانه را مگر زنجیر

" I sent a message to that Cashmerian idol, Why is my heart held captive under the curl of your ringlets ? She answered, Because your heart is distracted with love ; and the madman is not suffered to appear abroad without a chain."

Another Example.

زان مطرب مجلست زند دست بهم
کز باغ زمانه رم کند طایر غم
نی نی غلطم که دستهای مطرب
از شادی بزم بوسه گیرند بهم

" At your banquet that minstrel strikes her hands together, in order that she may drive away the bird of sorrow from the garden of delight. No, no, I am mistaken, for the hands of the minstrel, rejoicing at the feast, are kissing each other."

G

Te-já-he-lool a-rif تجاهل العارف is when the speaker is acquainted with a subject, but, pretending ignorance, sets forth that it is thus or thus, and relates other matters of a similar nature :

روز گار آشفته تر يازلف تو يا گار من
درہ کمتر يا دهانت يا دل افگار من

" Which is most disordered, your ringlets or my mind ? Which is smallest, your mouth or my afflicted heart ?"

Another Example from Jami.

عارض است اين يا قمر يا لاله' حمر است اين
يا شعاع شمس يا آئينه' دلها است اين
چشم تو جاد و است يا آهو است يا صياد خلق
يا دو بادام سيه يا نرگس شهلا است اين
قامت است اين يا الف يا سرو يا نخل مراد
يا مشگر گلدسته' باغ جنان آر است اين
زلف يا قلاب يا زنجير يا مشک ختن
سنبل تر برشن يا عنبر سارا است اين
يارب اين طاق است يا محراب يا قوس قزح
يا هلال عيد يا ابروي ماه ماست اين
حقه' لعل است يا سر چشمه آب حيات
يا دهن يا ميم يا طوطي شکر خاست اين
يارب اين خورشيد تابانست يا ماه تمام
يا فرشته يا پري يا شوخ بي پرواست اين
کوي تو کعبه است يا خلد برين يا بوستان
يا گلستان ارم يا جنت الها وا است اين

طوطي شيرين زبان يا تهري باغ جنان
بلبل سي خانمان يا جامي شيدا است اين

" This is a face, or the moon, or a beautiful tulip ; or else the beams of the sun, or a mirror of hearts. Your eyes are enchantments, or a deer, or a hunter of mankind ; or else two black almonds, or two beautiful narcissuses. This is a human form, or an *alif*, or a cypress, or the tree of desire ; or perhaps a nosegay, an ornament of the garden of Eden. It is a ringlet, or a hook, or a chain, or else musk of Tartary; fresh spikenard bent upon a lily, or ambergris of Sana. Wonderful ! it is an arch, or an altar, or the rainbow ; or the festival new moon, or the eye-brow of my mistress. It is a casket of rubies, or the source of the fountain of immortality ; it is either a mouth, or a *meem*, or a sugar-pecking parrot. Astonishment ! this is either the glorious sun, or the full moon ; or an angel, or a fairy, or else it is my blithsome mistress. The street where thou dwellest is Caaba, or Paradise, or Eden, or the bower of Irem, or the mansions of the Blessed; whilst Jami may be compared to a sweet-tongued parrot, or a dove of the garden of Paradise, or a wandering nightingale."

Mo-bá-lé-géh مبالغه or hyperbole, is when the author exceeds the bounds of probability. Of this there are three species.

1. *Tub-leegh* تبليغ when the thing is possible both to reason and experience :

بینم چو با رقیبت روزي نشسته تنها

از فکر آن نیاید خوابم بدیدہ شبها

" Should I behold you but one day in private with my rival,
such a sight would deprive my eyes of rest for many nights."

2. *Igh-rák* اغراق when the thing is possible, but not 'probable :

در روز هجر هرچند بیحد دهي شرابم

دور از تو شب نیایب اصلا بدیدہ خوابم

" In the day that you are absent, should they drench me ever so
much with wine, being distant from you, sleep would not
visit my eyes for an instant."

3. *Ghoo-loo* غلو when the assertion is absolutely impossible :

بعزم گردشش آن گرم رقتار

بگردد گرد گردون همچو پرگار

هوانا کردہ راهش التیا مي

که یابد دورہٴ او انتظا مي

" When that swift courser undertakes his journey, he revolves round
the sphere like a pair of compasses ; and so rapid is his way,
that the air cannot unite again before he has completed his
circuit."

Luff-ó-nusher لف و نشر in Arabic signifying twisting and un-
folding, is when some properties are described, and then others introduced ; but it is left to the discernment of the hearer to connect
them properly together.

Example from the Shahnameh.

بروز نبرد آن یل ارجمند
بشمشیر و خنجر بگرز وکمند
برید ودرید وشکست وبه بست
یلان را سرو سینه و پا و دست

" In the day of battle, that noble warrior, with sword, dagger,
club, and noose; cut, tore, broke, and bound that hero's head,
breast, feet, and hands."

Another Example, where no Arrangement is observed.

در باغ شد از قد ورخ و زلف تویاب
گلبرگ تری سرو سهی سنبل سیراب

" In comparison with your stature, your cheeks and your ringlets,
there cannot be found in the garden, either fresh rose leaves,
or a straight cypress, or fresh spikenard."

Muz-hé bé-ké-lá mee مذهب کلامی is when the Poet brings
proof of his assertion :

آن باد یه که منزل جانان است
نزد دل من به ازبسي بستان است
زیرا که بود مراد جانم آنجا
هرجا که بود مراد بهتران است

" That wilderness, wherein is situated the dwelling of my mistress,
in my estimation, is preferable to a garden; because there is

the wish of my heart, and that place is most desirable on which the affections are fixed."

Cowl-bá mu-jeb قول با موجب is when there occur in conversation, words which the hearer comprehends differently from the intention of the speaker, and which words will bear a double interpretation :

رقیب گفت که افتاده ام مرا بردار
دعاش کردم و گفتم خدات بردارد

" My rival said, I have fallen, lift me up ; I blessed him, and said, May God lift you up (or take you to himself !)"

Sy-ák-ool-á-dád سیاق الاعداد is when the Author uses several subjects, each of which has a distinct signification, but to which one property will apply generally, as in the last hemistich of the following distich of Ameer Khusro :

مطربا سوي چمن وقت گل آهنگ توکو
صوت تو نغمه تو بربط تو چنگ تو کو

" Oh minstrel ! where are your exertions in the garden, during the season of the rose ? Where are your notes, your song, your harp, and your lute ?"

Tun-seek us-se-fát تنسیق الصفت is when he uses contrary properties, as they occur, without any order or regularity :

كان هنر مضكان ادب معدن كرم
بحر حيا جهان سخا مركز و قار

" The mine of art, the seat of order, the mine of munificence; the
sea of modesty, the world of liberality, the centre of dignity."

Ir-sál ul me-sul ارسال المثل is when the Poet introduces one
example into each distich :

و صل هرچند میسر دلم اندر طلب است
كوزه هرچند پر آبست ولي خشك لب است

" Notwithstanding so many interviews, my heart is still desirous
of more ; as the flagon, however full it may be of water, has
nevertheless dry lips."

Ir-sál ul me-se-layn ارسال المثلين is when the Poet introduces
two similes into every distich :

نصيحت همه عالم چو باد در قفس است
بگوش مردم نادان چو اب در غربال

" Advice from all the world, is like wind in a cage. In the ear of
the ignorant, it is like water in a sieve."

Te-dá-rook تدارك is when the Poet commences with words
that the hearer imagines to be satirical ; but when he listens to the
remainder of the sentence, he perceives the whole to be praise :

مدح تو بگفتند و نخواهم كه بگويند
زان روي كه مدح تو زاند ازه برون است

" They speak in your praise; but I do not wish them to speak, because your praise is beyond measure."

Ta-uj-joob تعجب is when the Poet introduces or expresses himself with amazement:

نيستي ديوانه براتش چرا غلطي همي
نيستي پروانه گرد شمع چون جولان كني

" You are not a madman, why will you roll upon fire? You are not a moth, why do you flutter round the candle?"

Jum-má ó tuf-reek ó tuk-seem جمع و تفريق و تقسيم

1. *Jum-ma* is when the Poet brings together several subjects, having one general property:

فقر و كنج و خمول راحت دان
شهرت و مال و جاه آفت دان

" Know that poverty, retirement, and obscurity, are comforts; whilst fame, riches, and dignities, are to be considered as misfortunes."

2. *Tuf-reek* when the Poet separates two subjects which explain one another, although there is no connection between them.

Example from Hafez.

دست ترا بابر كه آرد شبيه كرد
كين بدره بدره بارد و آن قطره قطره

" Who can compare your head to the clouds, since this showers
  bags of money, whilst the other gives only drop by drop ?"

Tuk-seem is when the Poet, in a hemistich or distich, recites
several particulars; and afterwards, in another hemistich or distich,
introduces some others in connection with them, and assigns each
to each regularly :

راضيم از عشق و می زانکه نيند آشنا
آن بدل بو الهوس و اين بلب پارسا

" I am pleased with love and wine, because they are not friends :
  neither love with the libidinous, nor wine with the lips of the
  pious man."

Jummá má tuf-reek جمع مع تغريق is when the Author unites
several particulars in one comparison, and then separates them with
contrary epithets :

جاي خصمت چو جاي تست رفيع
آن تو تخت و آن دشمن دار

" The station of your enemy is as exalted as yours : yours is a
  throne, and his is a gibbet."

Jummá má tuk-seem جمع مع التقسيم is when the Poet, in a
hemistich or a distich, first uses words collectively, and again separately in another hemistich or distich :

غم دو چیز مرا دو چیز سپرد

دیده را آب و سینه را زنگار

" To two things that belonged to me, sorrow gave me two other
things; water to my eyes, and exceeding pain to my breast."

And it may happen that he first uses them separately, and then
collectively, as in the following verses:

با دوستان بدی تو و بادشمنان نکو

این خوی تست وه چکند کس بخوی تو

" You are bad to your friends, and good to your enemies: this is
your nature, and who can change nature ?"

Jum-má má tuf-reek ó *tuk-seem* تقسیم و تفریق مع جمع is
when the Author first uses several things collectively, in one signification, and then discriminates them :

همچو چشم تو نگر است لبش

این باب آن بلو لوی شهوار

آب این تیره آب آن روشن

این که گریه آن که گفتار

" Her lips abound, like my eyes; these with tears, and those with
royal pearls : but the water of these is turbid, and the water
of those is bright; mine are exhibited in weeping, her's in
speech."

Hoosn te-lub طلب حسن is when the Speaker wants to say

something in praise of the person, so as to give him satisfaction, without trespassing the bounds of decorum :

خسروا باز مانه در جنگم
كه بهم ميكند اردم هموار
چه بود گرکف توبردارد
ز ميان من و زمانه غبار

" O king! I am at variance with the world, because I am always living uncomfortably. How easy would it be for thy hand to remove the strife that is between us !"

Mud-hé-mo-wuj-jeh مدح موجه called also *Is-tem-bá* استنباع is when the Poet exalts the character of his patron, by alluding to other virtues besides what are directly set forth, and thereby bestowing double praise :

آن كند كوشش تو براعدا
كه كند بخشش تو بر دينار

" Your gallant actions have the same effect upon your enemies, as your munificence hath upon money."

It-té-rád اطراد is praising any one along with his ancestors, in genealogical order :

Example from Abool Férâj Roomee.

ترتيب ملك و قاعده دين ورسم داد
عبد المجيد احمد عبد الصمد نهاد

" He governed the kingdom, regulated the empire, and distributed justice; Abdool Mujeed, the son of Ahmed, the son of Adbus-se-mud."

Ké-lá-mé já-má جامع کلام is when the Poet treats on morality, philosophy, or worldly delights :

نصيحتي کنمت یاد گير و در عمل آر
كه این حدیث ز پیر طریقتم یاد است
مجو درستي عهد از جهان سست نهاد
كه این عجوزه عروس هزار داماد است
هرگز نبود دمی حضور و طربم
هر لحظه شون زیاده رنج و تعبم
هر دم الهي دگر رسد بي سببم
القصه من از طالع خود در عجبم

" I give a piece of advice, remember and act accordingly; since it is a saying which I recollect to have heard from a man of piety, Look not for the exact performance of an engagement, from a world whose principles are relaxed; for this widow hath been the bride of a thousand husbands. I have never enjoyed a moment of pleasure and satisfaction; every instant being an increase of sorrow and distress. In short, I am astonished at my own destiny."

Ul-huj-lo-yu-rá-do-bé-hil-jud-deh الهزل یراد به الجد is when what seems to be only a stroke of humour, is really truth :

مردم مشهد بسي نوشند مي شكفتا كسي
شكفتمش آن هست مي وقي خورند ايشان بسي .

" The people of Meshed drink a great deal of wine, said a certain
person. I answered him, in truth that is wine; but they also
drink a great deal of what has been cast up by others."

This distich, although given as a joke, yet contains a philosophi-
cal remark; because the people of Meshed drink a great deal of قي
which is honey, or the vomit of bees.

There is a story, that an old woman came to Mohammed, and
besought him to pray to God to admit her into paradise. He told
her, that old women did not enter there; upon which she departed
in tears and lamentation. But at length the Prophet ordered one
of his companions to tell her, that no old women enter paradise,
because God hath promised to restore them to youth, before he
removes them to the mansions of bliss.

Tál-meeh تلميح literally signifies using something savoury; and
is when the Author alludes to some popular story or verse:

Allusion to a Story.

نور چشما بي شكل ، ويت به بستان حال من
شكشته همچون حالت يعقرب در بيت الحزن

" O light of my eyes! when the garden of my condition is deprived of the rose of thy countenance, my state becomes like Jacob in the house of mourning."

Allusion to Verses.

پیش من حاصل کونین بود چون یك جو

مزرع چرخ چرا بینم و داس مه نو

" In my estimation, the harvest of both worlds would be equivalent to a barley-corn ; why should I behold the field of sky, and the sickle, the new moon ?"

This alludes to the following Distich of Hafiz :

مزرع سبز فلك دیدم و داس مه نو

یادم از کشته خویش آمد و هنگام درو

" When I survey the field of azure sky, and the sickle, the new moon ; I recollect my own field, and the season of harvest."

A-á-trá zool ké-lá-mé kub-bul ul ét mám اعتراض الکلام قبل الا تمام called also *Hushoo* حشو is when the Poet commences a subject, and, before the distich is concluded, brings in something else, (without which the sense would be complete,) and then proceeds with the original subject. Of this there are three species.

1. *Hosh-oo Khe-be-eh* حشو قبیح when there is introduced a superfluous word, as in the following example :

رای تو همچو شمس منیر است و روشن است

ذات تو همچو کوه حلیم است و برد بار

" Your understanding, like the sun, is light and bright ; your tem-
per resembles a mountain, in patience and suffering."

Here روشن after منير بردبار after حليم and are tautology.

Hush-oo me-te wasset حشو مطوسط is when the words, although
superfluous to the sense, do not injure the verse, so that their being
there or not is a matter of indifference; such as اي آفتاب مرتبه
in the following distich :

در جنب راي روشن تو نور آفتاب
اي آفتاب مرتبه نوريست مستعار

" By the side of your enlightened mind, (who equal the sun in
dignity,) the light of the sun is a borrowed light."

Hush-oo me-leeh حشو مليح is when the superfluous words are
introduced to embellish the style :

تيغت كه باد سينه خصمت نيام او
در دست تو چو با اسد الله ذوالفقار

" Your sword, (may the bosom of your enemy be its scabbard !)
in your hand, may it resemble Zoolfecar* in the hand of the
lion of God (Ali) !"

Here the words باد سينهٔ خصمت نيام او are superfluous.

* Name of the famous two-edged sword of Ali.

Il-te-fát التفات literally signifies looking from one side to another ; and, in poetry, means changing the personal pronouns.

Changing from the Second to the Third Person.

جانان زفراق تو دلم پر خون شد
وزیاد رخت سرشک من گلگون شد
القصه بکام دشمنان گشتم دوست
یکبار نه پرسید که حالت چون شد

" O my beloved ! on account of thy absence, my heart was full of blood ; and, at the remembrance of thy cheek, my tears were red : in short, I was in the condition of her enemies, whilst my friend did not once enquire after me."

From the Third to the Second Person.

گر یار طبیب درد من نیست
دردا که امید زیستن نیست
بیمار ترا به تند رستی
جز ناله میان پیرهن نیست

" If my friend is not my physician, alas there is no hope of life ! your patient came to you in full health, but now his garments contain nothing but a sigh."

From the First to the Second Person.

پیشتر بر خودم یقینی بود
که دلم هیچ دلستان نبرد

تو بردي همه يقين مرا
بطريقي که‌کس کمان نبرد

" Formerly I was confident, within myself, that no mistress could
deprive me of my heart : you bereft me of all my confidence,
in such a manner as to leave no doubt with any one."

From the First to the Third Person.

کفتمش عيد است آن رخسار و ابر و ماه عيد
کفت آري روشن است اين حال پيش اهل ديد

" I said to her, These cheeks are a festival, and your eyebrow is the
festival moon. She replied, Yes, this matter is very clear to
those who can see."

From the Second to the First Person.

بي روي تو شكر هزار كلذار بود
در چشم عطايي همه چون خار بود
نبود چو غم هجر مرا هيچ غمي
هر چند غم زمانه بسيار بود

" Deprived of your countenance, if there were a thousand flower-
beds in the eyes of Atta-y, they would all resemble thorns :
I can suffer no grief equal to that occasioned by my separation
from you, although I have experienced many worldly sor-
rows."

From the Second to the First Person.

دلي كه عاشق و صابر بود مگر سنگ است

ز عشق تا بصبوري هزار فرسنگ است

چه تربيت شنوم من چه مصلحت بينم

مرا كه چشم بساقي و گوش برچنگ است

" The heart that can contain both love and patience, is not a heart, but a stone; there are a thousand pharsangs distance between love and patience: what discipline shall I adopt, what advice shall I pursue, my eyes being fixed on the cup-bearer, and my ears attention to the harp?"

Is-te-á-reh استعار literally signifies borrowing, and in Rhetoric is when the Author, instead of the proper sense, borrows another meaning: but it is requisite that the resemblance be striking, and that the change contributes to the embellishment of the composition. The *is-te-á-reh*, or simile, is a species of *mejaz* or metaphor.

Mejáz مجاز The difference between the simile and the metaphor is, that, when the borrowed word is not the governing noun, it is called a metaphor; such as in the instance of valour, a man is called a lion: and if the borrowed word governs something else in the sentence, it is a simile; and in this case it is an expletive, because here the governing noun, and the noun governed, are one and the same thing, such as شكل مراد the flower of hope; باغ اميد the garden of hope; meaning in fact nothing but hope:

چشم دولت ز سواد قلت شکشته منير
باغ دانش ز سحاب کرمت کشنه نضير

" The eyes of fortune obtained light through the ink of his pen;
the garden of wisdom was refreshed by the clouds of his munificence."

Mo-te-zád متضاد is when the Author uses in a sentence words
of opposite significations; as hot and cold, long and short, black
and white:

بي روي همچو روزت وبى زلف چون شبت
صبحم چو شام نور چو نار است و گل چو خار

" Without your face, which resembles day, and your ringlets (jetty)
like night, morning appears to me like evening, light seems
fire, and the rose a thorn."

The following hemistich of Sulman is divided into two opposite
senses:

هشیار درون رفت و برون آمد مست

" Prudence went in, and Debauchery departed."

Another Example from the Shulestán of Fut-tá-hee.

برخاست نشاط زود و غم دیر نشست

" Mirth rose quickly; Sorrow sat late."

I 2

There is another species of *Mo-te-zád*, where the four elements are brought together.

Example from Abool Fé-ráj Roomee.

بادي كه در آيي به تنم همچونفس
ناري كه بسوزي دل خلقان بهوس
آبي كه بيتوزنده توان بودن و بس
خاكی كه به تست بازكشت همه كس

" Thou art air, that enters my body like breath ; thou art fire, that
    consumes the hearts of mankind with desire; thou art water,
    without which life cannot be sustained ; thou art earth, to
    which all nature must return."

Ee-hám-te-zád تضاد ايهم is when two words bear two meanings
that are not opposite in one acceptation, although they are so when
taken in another sense.

گل بخنديد تا هوا بگريست

" The rose laughed (or expanded), from the time that the air wept
    (or produced rain)."

Mo-rá-a-tun ne-zeer مراعاة تنظير called also *te-nà-soob* تناسب
is when the Author unites things that have affinity, such as the sun
and the moon, the rose and the nightingale, bow and arrow, &c.

Another species of *té-na-soob* is when the beginning and the end
of a sentence have a relative meaning :

ز هجر و وصل تو در حيرتم چه چاره كنم
نه در برابر چشمي نه غايب از نظري

" In your absence and in your presence I am distracted, what remedy shall I procure? You are neither before my eyes, nor
hidden from my sight."

Of the nature of *tenásoob* is *ei-há-mee tenásoob* ابهام تناسب
which is using a word with two significations, one of which is
suitable to the occasion, and the other not:

اي آهوي كناوك انشكن مست
يك تير بود زآهوان شصت

" O lascivious fawn, thrower of darts! one arrow from a fawn is
equal to sixty."

Here the word *shust* is intended to express the number sixty,
and not the thumb-stall of an archer.

Hoos-ne mut-lá حسن مطلع is when the Poet exerts himself in
the *mutlá* of a *ghuzel* or *káseedeh*, so as to fix the hearer's attention, and excite his curiosity for the catastrophe.

Be-rá-ul-é is-teh-lál براعت استهلال is when the Poem opens
with an allusion to the subject; as Jami in the commencement of
Leila Mujnoon:

اي خاك تو تاج سر بلندان
مجنون تو عقل هو شمندان

محجوب ترا نهار ليلي
مكشوف ترا سها سهيلي

" O God ! the dust of thy threshold is the crown of the mighty;
thy foolishness is the understanding of the wise : to those
from whom thou art hidden, day is night ; whilst with them
to whom thou art revealed, Soha * is as conspicuous as Cano-
pus."

Hoos-né muk-tá حسن مقطع is when the Poet exerts himself
in the concluding verses, and ends with something striking, in order
that the reader may leave off with satisfaction, and be induced to
excuse any inaccuracies which may have occurred in the course of
the poem. In the *ká-see-deh*, the *hoos-ne muk-tá* is generally used
in imploring blessing :

تا بود شورنده آب و تا بود سوزنده نار
تا بود پوینده باد و تا بود پاینده طین
باد اقبالت مدام و باد ایامت بکام
باد گرد ونت موافق بادیزدانت معین

" As long as water rageth, and as long as fire burneth ; as long as
wind moveth, and as long as the earth remaineth firm ; may
your good fortune continue, and your reign be happy ! may
your stars be propitious, having God for your support !"

* An obscure star in the constellation of the Greater Bear.

PART II.

PROSODY.

PART II.

P R O S O D Y.

عروض

THE word *Sheir* شعر literally signifies knowing and comprehending, and technically is used to express verse, or a sentence having sense, measure, and rhyme. A sentence, without measure, is not
verse; nor is measure, without metre and sense, poetry. It is not
lawful to call either the Koran or the Hadees poetry, although
verse accidentally occurs in them.

Since *Sheir* signifies a measured sentence, and every measure requiring a standard for ascertaining its quantity, it follows, that whosoever engages in the subject of poetry, either as composer or critic,
should necessarily be acquainted with the rules of prosody, or that
art by which the quality of the metre is discovered. Khaleel Ben
Ahmed Basaree was the first person who reduced prosody to rule.

This art is called *Arouz* عروض, or the art of measuring or scanning a sentence by one of the established scales of metre; whatever corresponds with one of these metres, is said to be in measure. The term for scanning is *Tucktea* * تقطيع.

A verse is scanned by separating its component words, in such a manner that every quantity thereof correspond in measure with the feet of that metre in which the verse is composed. In scanning the number of letters, the vowels and consonants are to be considered, but a similarity in letters and in accents is not required; for example, the words طوطي and بلبل are of the measure فَعْلُنْ. But every letter that is sounded is to be reckoned in scanning, although it be not written; and, on the contrary, every written letter that is not sounded, is not to be accounted of any value. And because scanning is founded on the sound, and not on the writing, the number of letters in one hemistich will often exceed those in another hemistich, although they are both of one measure.

Example.

خاص بمجلس كرم اهل سرور نشست
نخواست كه خوان چه خوان خان خواست خوان سه دو خوان سه دوخوان

Scanned thus:

لس‌خاص كرم‌بمج وراهلي نشست سر
فَعِلَاتْ مُفَاعِلُنْ فَعِلَاتَنْ مُفَاعِلُنْ

---

* *Tucktea* literally signifies pulling to pieces.

4

Scanned thus :

كه‌بخاس   سخاچخا   دسخاخا   دخاسخا

فَعِلَاتُنْ   مُفَاعِلُنْ   فَعِلَاتُنْ   مُفَاعِلُنْ

Here the first hemistich has 22, and the second 43 letters. It is to be observed, that Prosodians write the نون تنوين (or ن of nunnation) at full length, in order that the orthography may be conformable to the pronunciation, and that there may be no doubt.

Observations on the Letters ا *and* و *and* ي.

When ا and و have their appropriate vowels, the former is lengthened by extending the *Futteh*, and the latter by extending the *Zum* ; and when this is the case, the pronunciation is the same as if the letters were doubled :

Thus,

آمد ⎫
         ⎬ are pronounced ⎧ اامد ⎫ of the measure
آید ⎭   ⎩ اايد ⎭ of فَعْلُنْ

and

داود ⎫
         ⎬ are pronounced ⎧ داوود ⎫ of the measure
طاوس ⎭   ⎩ طاووس ⎭ of فَعْلَانْ

The first ا and و are considered accented, and the last quiescent.

The ى is suppressed to supply the place of *Kussir*, and for the short vowel gives a long tone, as in من بيدل where the *Kussir* being extended after ن the letter ى is to be sounded long; and in scanning this, ى would be written in this form مني بيدل in measure مَفَاعِيْلُنْ.

This ى is called بطني or hidden. And in this manner, in many Arabic words, ا and و and ى are sounded without being written, such as in الله and هذا and ذلكله and به &c.

Letters marked with a *Tushdeed* are also repeated, as خرّم and فرّخ which are in the measure فَعْلُنْ and, in scanning, they write two letters, the first quiescent, and the other accented in this manner خررم and فررخ.

Of the Letters ا *and* و *and* ه *and* ى *when written but not sounded.*

This ا is a conjunction occurring in the middle of an hemistich, when it receives the accent of the preceding letter, and the ا is not sounded; on which account it is called الف وصل or *Alif conjunctive,* because it seems to unite in sound the preceding and the subsequent letters. As for example:

روز سيغي سيه از كاكل مشكين توشد

In scanning this, ا is not sounded.

3

روزسيغي سيهزكا كلـمشكي نتـشد

فَأَعِلاَتَنْ فَعِلاَتَنْ فَعِلاَتَنْ فَعِلُنْ

But if *Alif* is sounded, it is not omitted in scanning; as in the following hemistich :

بود فرياد سيغي در غمت از دست تنهائي

Scanned thus,

بودفريا دسيغيدر غمتازدس تتنهائي

مَفَاعِيلُنْ مَفَاعِيلُنْ مَفَاعِيلُنْ مَفَاعِيلُنْ

The letter و is of three kinds واوعطف being that which occurs between two words as a conjunction; such as دل وجان and اين و آن In the Persian language, it generally happens that the letter preceding this و is marked with a *Zum*, and then the و is not sounded; as in the following hemistich :

دل و دلد ارو صبر و طاقت كو

In scanning this, و is not written.

دلدلدا رصبرطا قتكو

فَعِلاَتَنْ مَفَاعِلُنْ فَعْلُنْ

But if the و is sounded, it is not omitted in scanning ; thus

گل و مل مي بايد و ديد اريار

Scanned thus,

داريار   بايدودي   ڭلوملسي

فَاعِلَاتْ   فَاعِلَاتَنْ   فَاعِلَاتَنْ

Another called واوبيان ضمه is used to express the accent and complete the word, (because no sound can be expressed by less than two letters;) such as همچو and چو and دو and تو

It generally happens that this و is not sounded; as in the following hemistich:

همچو تو كو درد و سرا ديشكري ·

Scanned thus,

ديڭري   دردسرا   همچتتو

فَاعِلُنْ   مُفْتَعِلُنْ   مُفْتَعِلُنْ

But if it is sounded, it is not omitted in scanning; as for example,

ديشكري در دو سراكو مثل تو

Scanned thus,

مثلتو   دوسراكو   ديشكريدر

فَاعِلُنْ   فَاعِلَاتَنْ   فَاعِلَاتَنْ

Another called وا و اشبام ضمه is that which occurs after accented with a *Futteh*, but the *Futteh* of خ is not pure, as it partakes somewhat of the *Zum*.

Ishmám اشپام literally signifies causing to smell ; and therefore this is called *Ishmam Zummeh,* or *smelling of Zum.*

Example.

خواب و خورنخوا جهٔ من خوش بود

خاب‌خري   خاجي‌من   خش‌بود

مُفْتَعِلُنْ   مُفْتَعِلُنْ   فَاْعِلُنْ

The letter ه, when used to express an accent, is called بيان حركت and occurs to shew that the letter preceding it is accented, either with a *Futteh,* as خنده and كربه or else with a *Kussir,* as كه and چه and سه &c. Therefore, if this ه occurs in the middle of an hemistich, and is not sounded, it is omitted in scanning. Thus :

كري‌كردي   خندكردي

فَاْعِلَاتَنْ   فَاْعِلَاتَنْ

But if it is sounded with a *Kussir* in its stead, they use ي . Thus,

كربي‌من   خندي‌او

مُفْتَعِلُنْ   مُفْتَعِلُنْ

If it occurs at the end of an hemistich, it is reckoned ي as a quiescent letter. Thus,

غنچه پيش دهنت لب بسته

Scanned thus,

بسته دهنت‌لب غنیج‌پیشی

فَعْلُنْ فَعْلَاتَنْ فَاعِلَاتَنْ

The ه in بسته is equivalent to ن in فَعْلُنْ : and it sometimes happens that this ه, in the middle of an hemistich, corresponds with a quiescent letter in scanning; as for example,

خنده چه کنی بشکریه ییی‌من

Scanned thus,

ییی‌من کنی‌بشکر خندیچ

فَعُولُنْ مُفَاعِلُنْ مُفْعُولُ

The letter یای ساکن or quiescent, is when it precedes an accented *Alif*, and is not sounded.

سیغی از عشق اوجدا منشین

In scanning this, ی is not written.

منشین قاوجدا سیف‌ازعش

فَعلَاتْ مُفَاعِلُنْ فَاعِلَاتَنْ

Some consider this form as a syncope, and say that the accent of the ١ is transferred to the ی, the *Alif* being struck out.

And they scan the above hemistich thus,

منبشین   قـاوجدا   سيغيزعش

فَعِلَاتْ   مُغَاعِلُنْ   فَاعِلَاتُنْ

But if ي is sounded, it is not omitted in scanning; as for example,

هست سيغني از دعاگويان مجو آز اراو

Scanned thus,

زاراو   يامـجواا   ازدعاكو   هست سيغني

فَاعِلُنْ   فَاعِلَاتُنْ   فَاعِلَاتُنْ   فَاعِلَاتُنْ

Of ن quiescent, and of some other Letters that are written; with their Treatment in Scanning.

It is to be observed, that ن is quiescent when it occurs after any letter of the class called *Muddeh* مد which are ا and و and ي quiescent, preceded by a letter accented with their proper vowels, *Zum, Futteh,* and *Kussir,* as in the words چين and جان and چون when these occur in the middle of an hemistich ن is omitted in scanning, as in the following hemistich :

چون كنم و جان كنم و چون روم

Scanned thus,

چوكنم   جاكنم   چي‌لوم

فَاعِلُنْ   فَاعِلُنْ   فَاعِلُنْ

And, if this ن occurs at the end of an hemistich, it is considered
as a quiescent letter; thus:

اي قد دلجوي تو سرو روان

اي‌فدي‌دل   جوي‌توسر   وي‌روان

فَاعِلَاتَنْ   فَاعِلَاتَنْ   فَاعِلَاتْ

This letter ن in the word روان corresponds with ت in فَاعِلَاتْ
But if the *muddeh* letter is not followed by a ن such as نار and
نور and نير; or if the last letter is ن not preceded by a *muddeh*,
such as امن and عون and عين; or if it is neither of these, such
as شكر and these two quiescents occur in the middle of an hemistich, in that case the second quiescent is accented; as in the
following example:

يارسو   امن‌جو   شكركو

فَاعِلُنْ   فَاعِلُنْ   فَاعِلُنْ

These are all in the measure of فَاعِلُنْ because, by the rules of
Prosody, two quiescents are not allowed in the middle of an hemistich, excepting ا and ن which, both together, stand for one quies-

cent, on account of the light sound of the *muddeh* letter (or *alif*)
along with the quiescent ن ; but if two quiescents occur at the end
of an hemistich, they are reckoned two quiescents ; as for example,

كوي يارو ملك امن وجاي شكر

All in the measure of فَاْعِلَاتْ without reckoning the conjunction و

If the *muddeh* letter is followed by two quiescent letters, such
as كارد and كوشت and كشتاسب in the middle of an hemistich,
and in scanning, these two quiescents correspond with an accented
letter, then the first quiescent is accented, and the second is rejected ; as for example,

كارد بركش كوشت بر كشتاسبرا

Scanned thus,

كاربركش   كوشبركش   تاسرا

فَاْعِلَاتَنْ   فَاْعِلَاتَنْ   فَاْعِلَنْ

But when two such quiescents correspond with two accented letters in the measure, then both the quiescents become accented ; as
for example,

رزم بود كارد جو بزم بود كوشت كو

L 2

Scanned thus,

رزم‌بود   کارد‌جو   بزم‌بود   گوشت‌کو
مُفْتَعِلُنْ   مُفْتَعِلُنْ   مُفْتَعِلُنْ   مُفْتَعِلُنْ

When three quiescents occur together at the end of an hemistich, the last is omitted in scanning, because in Prosody three quiescents can in no place come together.

تا چوسیغی بتوای شمع مرا سرگرمی است

Scanned thus,

تاچسیغی   بت‌ای‌شم   عمراسر   گرمیس
فَاعِلَاتُنْ   فَعِلَاتُنْ   فَعِلَاتُنْ   فَعِلَانْ

The Component Parts of Verse.

Verse, in the language of the Arabian and Persian Prosodians, is composed of *Urkan* ارکان and *Ussool* اصول or feet and syllables.

Syllables are of three kinds, *Sebnb* سبب *Wetud* وتد and *Fáseleh* فاصله each divided into *Khefeef* خفیف and *Sekeel* ثقیل or soft and hard breathing.

1st kind. Soft breathing is composed of an accented and a quiescent letter, as لَمْ In the hard breathing, both the letters are accented as اَرَ

2d kind. Soft breathing is composed of two accented letters followed by a quiescent, as عَلَيْ In the hard breathing, the quiescent letter is in the middle, as رَأْس

3d kind. Soft breathing is composed of three accented letters and a quiescent, with the sign of nunnation, as جَبَل In the hard breathing there are four accented letters, and the last is quiescent, as سِكَّة

Of the Ur-kan اركان or Standards of Verse.

All the forms of metre are taken from the verb فعل and its derivations; and every species of verse is comprized in the eight following standards:

فَعُولُنْ — 1 Fá-oo-loon,

— — ◡

فَاعِلُنْ — 2 Fá-a-loon,

— ◡ —

مَفَاعِيلُنْ — 3 Mu-fá-ee-loon,

— — — ◡

مُسْتَفْعِلُنْ — 4 Moos-tuf-a-loon,

— ◡ — —

مُفَاعَلَتُنْ — 5 Mu-fá-a-la-toon,

— ◡ ◡ — ◡

مُتَفَاعِلُنْ — 6 Mu-ta-fá-a-loon

— ◡ — ◡ ◡

فَاعِلَاتُنْ — 7 Fá-a-lá-toon,

— ◡ — —

مَفْعُولَاتُ — 8 Muf-oo-lá-to.

◡ — — —

Of the Misra and its Component Parts.

It is generally allowed, that a verse cannot consist of less than a
distich formed of two hemistichs; and half the distich is called
misru مصراع because that word literally signifies a door of two
folds; and the resemblance between a distich and a door of two
folds is in this, that in the same manner as with a door of two folds
you may open or shut which you please without the other; and
when you shut both together, it is still but one door: so also of a
distich, you may read which of the hemistichs you please without
the other, and when you read both together, they will form one
distich. The first foot, of the first hemistich, is called *Sudr* صدر
and the last foot thereof *Arooz* عروض Of the second hemistich,
the first foot is called *Ibtedá* ابتدا and the last *Zurb* ضرب The
intermediate feet of both have the general name *Hushoo* حشو The
meaning of *Sudr* is the *first*, and *Ibteda* signifies *commencement*;
the first beginning the distich, as the other does the second hemistich. The last foot of the first hemistich is called *Arooz*, signifying the *pole of a tent*; for as the pole is the support of the tent, so
is the distich founded on this prop; for until this foot is determined,
the hemistich is not complete, nor its measure known.' The last
foot of the second hemistich is called *Zurb*, i. e. *of one kind*, or
alike, it resembling the *Arooz* in that both are at the end of an
hemistich, and that the conclusion of verses are alike by the obser-

vance of rhyme. *Hushoo* is the stuffing of a cushion, and, on account of their situation, the intermediate feet are so called.

Feet are either *Sálem* سالم or *Gháir sálem* غير سالم perfect or imperfect. The perfect foot is that in which the verse is originally composed, without excess or diminution. The imperfect foot is that wherein some change has happened, either by adding something to it, or taking something from it; as for example, if in the word مفاعلين between ل and ن you introduce an Alif ا and read مفاعيلن or if from the same word you take away ن and the accent of the ل and say مفاعيل The imperfect foot is called *Mo-za-huf* مزاحف and the alteration is called *Zeháf* زحاف derived from زحف *Zehuf*, literally signifying departing from its original intention; as we say *Sehmé Záhif* سهم زاحف an arrow that errs from the mark.

Of the Number of Bo-hoor بحور *or Metres.*

There are 19 Species of Metre, viz.

طويل	1 — Teweel,		هزج	6 — He-zuj,
مديد	2 — Me-deed,		رجز	7 — Re-juz,
بسيط	3 — Be-seet,		رمل	8 — Re-mul,
وافر	4 — Wá-fir,		منسرح	9 — Moon-se-reh,
كامل	5 — Ká-mil,		مضارع	10 — Mo-zá-ra,

مقتضب 11 — Mook-te-zub,	خفيف 16 — Khe-feef,
مجتث 12 — Mooj-tus,	مشاكل 17 — Mu-shá-kil,
سريع 13 — Se-ree-a,	متقارب 18 — Mu-te-ká-rib,
جديد 14 — Je-deed,	متدارك 19 — Mu-te-da-rik.
قريب 15 — Ke-reeb,	

Of these 19 measures, the five first are almost peculiar to the Arabians; very few Persian or Turkish Poets have used them, because not suited to the genius of these languages. The 14th, 15th, and 17th, are peculiar to Persian Poetry: but the other 11 species are used both in Arabic and in Persian.

Of the Ru-ba-ie, or Tetrastick.

The measure of the Ru-bá-ie رباعي (called also Du-by-tee دوبيتي and Tir-á-neh ترانه) is derived from the measure He-zuj هزج It was invented by the Persians. There are twenty-four kinds of the Ru-bá-ie, which are exhibited at the conclusion of the imperfect forms of versification.

The Perfect Forms of every Kind of Versification.

مَفَاعِيْلُنْ	مفاعيلن	مفاعيلن	مفاعيلن	هزج
مُسْتَفْعِلُنْ	مستفعلن	مستفعلن	مستفعلن	رجز
فَاعِلَاتُنْ	فاعلاتن	فاعلاتن	فاعلاتن	رمل
مُسْتَفْعِلُنْ	مَفْعُولَاتُ	مستفعلن	مفعولات	منسرح
مَفَاعِيْلُنْ	فَاعِلَاتُنْ	مفاعيلن	فاعلاتن	مضارع
مَفْعُولَاتُ	مُسْتَفْعِلُنْ	مفعولات	مستفعلن	مقتضب
مُسْتَفْعِلُنْ	فَاعِلَاتُنْ	مستفعلن	فاعلاتن	مجتث
مُسْتَفْعِلُنْ		مستفعلن	مَفْعُولَاتُ	سريع
فَاعِلَاتُنْ		فاعلاتن	مُسْتَفْعِلُنْ	جديد
مَفَا عِيْلُنْ		مفا عيلن	فَاعِلَاتُنْ	قريب
فَاعِلَاتُنْ		مُسْتَفْعِ لُنْ	فاعلاتن	خفيف
فَاعِلَاتُنْ		مَفَا عِيْلُنْ	مفاعيلن	مشاكل
فَعُوْلُنْ	فعولن	فعولن	نعولن	متقارب
فَاعِلُنْ	فاعلن	فاعلى	فاعلن	متدارك
مَفَاعِيْلُنْ	فعولن	مَفَاعِيْلُنْ	مفاعيلن	طويل
فَاعِلَاتُنْ	فَاعِلُنْ	فاعلاتن	فاعلن	مديد

M

بسيط	مُسْتَفْعِلُنْ فَاْعِلُنْ مستفعلن فاعلن
وافر	مُفَاْعِلَتُنْ مفاعلتن مفاعلتن مفاعلتن
كامل	مُتَفَاْعِلُنْ متفاعلن متفاعلن متفاعلن

Imperfect Forms.

هزج

مثمن مسبغ	مَفَاْعِيْلُنْ مفاعيلن مفاعيلن مَفَاْعِيْلَاْنْ
مثمن مقبوض	مَفَاْعِلُنْ مفاعلن مفاعلن مفاعلن
مثمن مقبوض مسبغ	مَفَاْعِلُنْ مفاعلن مفاعلن مَفَاْعِلَاْنْ
مثمن اشتر	فَاْعِلُنْ مَفَاْعِيْلُنْ فاعلن مفاعيلن
مثمن اخرب	مَفْعُوْلُ مَفَاْعِيْلُنْ مفعول مفاعيلن
مثمن اخرب مكفوف مقصور	مَفْعُوْلُ مَفَاْعِيْلُ مفاعيل مفاعيل
مثمن اخرب مكفوف محذوف	مَفْعُوْلُ مَفَاْعِيْلُ مفاعيل فَعُوْلُنْ
مثمن مكفوف محذوف	مَفَاْعِيْلُ مفاعيل مفاعيل فَعُوْلُنْ
مسدس مقصور	مَفَاْعِيْلُنْ مفاعيلن مَفَاْعِيْلُ
مسدس محذوف	مفاعيلن مفاعيلن فعولن
مسدس مكفوف مقصور	مفاعيل مفاعيل مَفَاْعِيْلْ
مسدس مكفوف محذوف	مَفَاْعِيْلُ مفاعيل نعولن

مفاعيلن	مُفَاعِلَنْ	مُفْعُوْلُ	مسدس اخرب مقبوض
مَفَاعِيْلُ	مفاعِلن	مفعولُ	مسدس اخرب مقبوض مقصور
فعولن	مفاعلن	مفعول	مسدس اخرب مقبوض محذوف
فعولن	مَفَاعِيلُ	مفعول	مسدس اخرب مكفوف محذوف
مفاعيلن	فاعلن	فَاعِلُنْ	مسدس اشتر
مَفَاعِيْلُ	فاعلن	مفعولن	مسدس اخرب اشتر مقصور

رجز

مُسْتَفْعِلُنْ مستفعلن مستفعلن مستفعلَانْ		مُسْتَفْعِلُنْ	منهن مدال
مفتعلن	مفتعلن مفتعلن	مُفْتَعِلُنْ	مثهن مطوى
مُفَاعِلُنْ	مفتعلن مفاعلن مُفْتَعِلُنْ	مثهن مطوي مخبون
مفتعلن	مفتعلن مفاعلن	مثهن مخبون مطوي مفاعلن
مفتعلن	مفتعلن	مفتعلن	مسدس مطوي
مفاعلن	مفاعلن	مفاعلن	مسدس مخبون

رمل

| فَاعِلِيَانْ | فاعلاتن | فاعلاتن | فَاعِلَاتُنْ | مثهن مسبغ |
| فعلاتن | فعلاتن | فعلاتن | فَعِلَاتُنْ | مثهن مخبون |

مثمن مقصور	فاعلاتن فاعلاتن فاعلاتن فَأَعِلَاتْ		
مثمن محذوف	فاعلاتن فاعلاتن فاعلاتن فَأَعِلُنْ		
مثمن مشكول	فَعَلَاتُ فاعلاتن فعلات فاعلاتن		
مثمن مشكول مسبع	فعلات فاعلاتن فعلات فاعليان		
مثمن مخبون مسبغ	فاعلاتن فَعَلَاتُنْ فعلاتن فعليان		
مثمن مخبون مقصور	فاءلاتن فعلاتن فعلاتن فَعَلَاتْ		
مثمن مخبون محذوف	فاعلاتن فعلاتن فعلاتن فعلُنْ		
مثمن مخبون مقطوع	فاعلاتن فعلاتن فعلاتن فَعْلُنْ		
مثمن مخبون مقطوع مسبغ	فاعلاتن فعلاتن فعلاتن نَعْلَانْ		
مسدس مقصور	فاعلاتن فاعلاتن فَأَعِلَاتْ		
مسدس محذوف	فاعلاتن فاعلاتن فَأَعِلُنْ		
مسدس مخبون مقصور	فاعلاتن نعلاتن فَعَلَاتْ		
مسدس مخبون محذوف	فاعلاتن فعلاتن فَعَلُنْ		
مسدس مخبون مقطوع	فاعلاتن فعلاتن فَعْلُنْ		
مسدس مخبون مقطوع مسبغ	فاعلاتن نعلاتن فَعْلَانْ		

منسرح

مثمن مطوي موقوف	مفتعلن فَأَعِلَاتُ مفتعلن فَأَعِلَاتْ
مثمن مطوي مكسوف	مفتعلن فاعلن مفتعلن فاعلن

مثمن مطوي مجدوع · مفتعلن فاعلات مفتعلن فَاْعْ

مثمن مطوي منحور · مفتعلن فاعلات مفتعلن فَعْ

مسدس مطوي · مفتعلن فاعلات مفتعلن

مسدس مطوي مقطوع · مفتعلن فَاْعَلَاْتُ مفعولن

مضارع

مثمن اخرب · مَفْعُوْلُ فَاْعِلَاْتَنْ مفعول فاعلاتن

مثمن اخرب مسبغ · مفعول فاعلاتن مفعول فَاْعِلِيَّاْنْ

مثمن اخرب مكفوف · مفعول فَاْعَلَاْتُ مَفَاْعِيْلُ فاعلاتن

مثمن اخرب مكفوف مقصور · مفعول فاعلات مفعول مفاعيل فَاْعِلَاْتْ

مثمن اخرب مكفوف محذوف · مفعول فاعلات مفاعيل فَاْعَلُنْ

مثمن مكفوف مقصور · مفاعيل فاعلاتُ مفاعيل فاعِلَاْت

مسدس اخرب مكفوف · مفعول فاعلات مفاعيلن

مقتضب

مثمن مطوي · فاعلاتُ مفتعلن فاعلاتُ مفتعلن

مثمن مطوي مقطوع · فاعلات مفعولن فاعلات مفعولن

مجتث

مثمن مخبون · مُفَاْعِلُنْ فَعِلَاْتَنْ مفاعلن فعلاتن

مثمن مخبون مسبغ	مفاعلن فعلاتن مفاعلن	فعلاتن مفاعلن	فَعِلَيَأنْ
مثمن مخبون مقصور	مفاعلن فعلاتن مفاعلن	فعلاتن مفاعلن	فعلن
مثمن مخبون محذوف	مفاعلن فعلاتن مفاعلن	فعلاتن مفاعلن	فعلن
مثمن مخبون مقطوع	مفاعلن فعلاتن مفاعلن	فعلاتن مفاعلن	فَعُلُنْ
مثمن مخبون مقطوع مسبغ	مفاعلن فعلاتن مفاعلن	فعلاتن مفاعلن	فَعْلأنْ

سريع

مطوي موتوف	مفتعلن	مفتعلن	فاعلات
مطوي مكسوف	مفتعلن	مفتعلن	فاعلن

جديد

مخبون	فاعلاتن	مفاعلن	فعلاتن

قريب

مكفوف	مفاعيل	مفاعيل	فاعلاتن
اخرب مكفوف	مفعول	مفاعيل	فاعلاتن

خفيف

مخبون	فعلاتن	فعلاتن	مفاعلن
مخبون مقصور	فاعلاتن	مفاعلن	فعلات

فَعِلن	مفاعلن	فاعلاتن	مخبون محذوف
فَعْلِ	مفاعلن	فاعلاتن	مخبون مقطوع
فعلان	مفاعلن	فاعلاتن	مخبون مقطوع مسبغ

مشا كل

مفاعيل	مفاعيل	فاعلات	مكفوف مقصور	.

متقارب

فعول	فعولن	فعولن	فعولن	مثمن مقصور
فَعَلْ	فعولن	فعولن	فعولن	مثمن محذوف
فعولن	فَعُلَنْ	فعولن	فَعُلُنْ	مثمن اثلم
نعلن	فعول	فَعُلَنْ	فعول	مثمن مقبوض اثلم

متدارك

فعلن	فعلن	فعلن	فعلن	مثمن مخبون
فعْلن	فعْلن	فعْلن	فعْلن	مثمن مقطوع
نعل	فاعلن	فَعَلْ	فاعلن	مثمن مخبون مقطوع

Forms of the Ru-ba-ie.

اوزان رباعي از شجرهٔ خرم

مفعولن	فاعلن	مفاعيلن	فاعُ
مفعولن	مفعول	مفاعيلن	فاعُ
مفعولن	فاعلن	مفاعيل	فَعَلْ
مفعولن	مفعولن	مفعولن	فاعُ
مفعولن.	مفعولن	مفعولن	فع
مفعولن	فاعلن	مفاعيلن	فع
مفعولن	مفعول	مفاعيل	فعول
مفعولن	مفعول	مفاعيلن	فع
مفعولن	مفعول	مفاعيل	فَعَلْ
مفعولن	مفعولن	نعلن	نَعْكُنْ
مفعولن	فاعلن	مفاعيل	فعول
مفعولن	مفعولن	مفعول	فعول

اوزان رباعي از شجرهٔ اخرب

مَفْعُولُ	مُفَاعِلُنْ	مَفَاعِيلُنْ	فَعْ
مفعول	مَفَاعِيلٌ	مفاعيلن	فَعْ

مفعول	مفاعيلن	مفعول	فَعَلْ
مفعول	مفاعيلن	مَفْعُولُنْ	فَعْ
مفعول	مفاعيلن	مفعول	فَعُولُ
مفعول	مفاعيل	مفاعيل	فعول
مفعول	مُفَاعِلُنْ	متاعيل	فَعَلْ
مفعول	مفاعلن	مفاعيل	فعول
مفعول	مفاعلن	مفاعيلن	فاعْ
مفعول	مفاعيل	مفاعيلن	فاعْ
مفعول	مفاعيل	مفاعيل	فَعَلْ
مفعول	مفاعيل	مفعولن	فاعْ

TABLE,

Shewing the Alterations of the Imperfect Forms from the Standards of Metre.

Explained in Page 77.

Names of Imperfect Forms.	Name of the Altered Feet.	Original Perfect Forms.	ALTERATIONS. Letters added.	ALTERATIONS. Letters and Points rejected.	Imperfect Forms.	Words substituted.
تسبيغ	مسبغ	مفاعيلتن	—		مفاعيلان	
تنقص	مقبوض	مفاعيلن		ي	مفاعلن	
شتر	اشتر	مفاعيلن		مي	فاعلن	
حرب	احرب	مفاعيلن		ير	فاعلن	
عكف	مكفوف	مفاعيلن		ن	مفاعيل	مفعول
قصر	مقصور	مفاعيلن		ي	مفاعي	
حذف	محذوف	مفاعيلن		لن	مفاعي	
خرم	اخرم	مفاعيلن		م	فاعيلن	مفعولن مفعولن

(—3d Standard—)

		4th		1st		3d	

Scansion of Perfect Forms.

هزج مثمن سالم

دلا وصف میان نازک جانان من گفتی
نکو گفتی حدیثی از میان جان من گفتی

نهن گفتی	زکی‌جانا	میانی‌نا	دلاوصفی
مفاعیلن	مفاعیلن	مفاعیلن	مفاعیلن

نهن گفتی	میانی‌جا	حدیثی‌از	نکوگفتی
مفاعیلن	مفاعیلن	مفاعیلن	مفاعیلن

هزج مسدس سالم

قناعت کنج آباد است اگرد انی
از و تا میتوانی رو نگرد انی

تگرد انی	ج‌ابادس	قناعتکن
مفاعیلن	مفاعیلن	مفاعیلن

نکرد انی	توانی‌رو	از و تا می
مفاعیلن	مفاعیلن	مفاعیلن

Scansion of Perfect Forms.

رجز مثمن سالم

تاكي غم دل گفتنم درخانه با ديوارها
خواهم زد از بيطاقتى فرياد دربازارها

ديوارها	درخانبا	دل گفتنم	تاكي غمي
مستفعلن	مستفعلن	مستفعلن	مستفعلن

بازارها	فريادبدر	بيطاقتي	خاهم زدز
مستفعلن	مستفعلن	مستفعلن	مستفعلن

رجز مسدس سالم

ساقي بعشرت كوش دردو ران گل
مگذار از كف جام تا پايان گل

دوران گل	رتكوشدر	ساقي بعش
مستفعلن	مستفعلن	مستفعلن

پايان گل	كف جامتا	مگداراز
مستفعلن	مستفعلن	مستفعلن

Scansion of Perfect Forms.

رمل مثمن سالم

شَکَل دل بردن که تو داري نباشد دلبري را

خواب بنديهاي چشمت کم بود جاد و گري را

شکل دلبر دن که تو دا ري نباشد دلبري را

فاعلاتن فاعلاتن فاعلاتن فاعلاتن

خاب بندي هاي چشمت کم بود جا دو گري را

فاعلاتن فاعلاتن فاعلاتن فاعلاتن

رمل مسدس سالم

اي نگارين روي دلبرزان مايي

رخ مکن پنهان چواندر جان مايي

اي نگاري روي دلبر زان مايي

فاعلاتن فاعلاتن فاعلاتن

رخ مکن هاچ اندر جان مايي

فاعلاتن فاعلاتن فاعلاتن

Scansion of Perfect Forms.

متقارب مثمن سالم

اگر سر و من درچمن جا بشکیرد
عجب باشد ار سرو بالا بشکیرد

بشکیرد	چمنجا	ومندر	اگرسر
فعولن	فعولن	فعولن	فعولن

بشکیرد	وبالا	شدرسر	عجببا
فعولن	فعولن	فعولن	فعولن

متقارب مسدس سالم

زدرد جدایی چنانم
که اززند کانی بجانم

چنانم	جدایی	زدردي
فعولن	فعولن	فعولن

بجانم	دکانی	کهاززن
فعولن	فعولن	فعولن

Scansion of Perfect Forms.

متدارك مثمن سالم

حسن و لطف ترا بنده شد مهرو مه

خط و خال ترا مشك چین خاك ره

حسن لط   في ترا   بند شد   مهرمه

فاعلن   فاعلن   فاعلن   فاعلن

خطاطخا   لي ترا   مشك چي   خاكره

فاعلن   فاعلن   فاعلن   فاعلن

طویل مثمن سالم

دلارام مارا گر بو عده و فا بودي

بنوعي بدي كاخر تسلي بها بودي

دلارا   مهاراگر   بوعده   وفابودي

فعرلن   مفاعيلن   فعولن   مفاعيلن

بنوعي بدي كاخر تسلي   بهابودي

فعولن   مفاعيلن   فعولن   مفاعيلن

Scansion of Perfect Forms.

مدید مثمن سالم

اي دل پردردرا لعل تو درمان شده
خاك پايت بنددرا چشمه حيوان شده

ماشده	لعل تودر	دردرا	اي دل پير
فاعلن	فاعلاتن	فاعلن	فاعلاتن

واشده	چشمه حي	بندرا	خاك پايت
فاعلن	فاعلاتن	فاعلن	فاعلاتن

بسيط مثمن سالم

اي با و صالت دلم شادان زدور فلك
هجر تویر خاطرم چون بر جراحت نمك

ري فلك	شاد ازدو	لتملم	اي باوصا
فاعلن	مستفعلن	فاعلن	مستفعلن

حت نمك	جوبرجرا	خاطرم	هجري تبر
فاعلن	مستفعلن	فاعلن	مستفعلن

Scansion of Perfect Forms.

وافر مثمن سالم

چه شد صنما که سوي کسي بچشم رضانمي نگري
زرسم جفانمي گذري طريق وفانمي سپري

چهشدصنما   کهسويکسي   بچشمرضا   نمينگري
مفاعلتن   مفاعلتن   مفاعلتن   مفاعلتن

زرسمجفا   نميگذري   طريقوفا   نميسپري
مفاعلتن   مفاعلتن   مفاعتن   مفاعتن

کامل مثمن سالم

نه دلش زرسم جفاگهي بغلط بسوي و فارود
نه وفاي او بد و صد جفاز دل بلاکش مارود

ندلشزرس   مجفاگهی   بغلطبسو   يوفارود
متفاعلن   متفاعلن   متفاعلن   متفاعلن

بوفاياو   بدصدجفا   زدليبلا   کشمارود
متفاعلن   متفاعلن   متفاعلن   متفاعلن

Scansion of Perfect Forms.

هزج مثمن مسبغ

بزاري ميد هم جان و نهى پرسد مرا جانان

مسلماني نميدانم كجا شد اي مسلمان

مراجانان	نمي‌پرسد	دهم‌جانو	بزاري‌مي
مفاعيلان	مفاعيلن	مفاعيلن	مفاعيلن

مسلمانان	كـخاشداي	نميدانم	مسلماني
مفاعيلان	مفاعيلن	مفاعيلن	مفاعيلن

هزج مثمن مقبوض

دلم برون شد ازغمت غمت زدل برون نشد

زبون شدم كه بود كوزدست غم زبون نشد

برونشد	غمت‌زدل	شدزغمت	دلم‌برو
مفاعلن	مفاعلن	مفاعلن	مفاعلن

ا بونشد	زدستغم	كه‌بودكو	زبوشدم
مفاعلن	مفاعلن	مفاعلن	مفاعلن

Scansion of Perfect Forms.

هزج مثمن مقبوض مسبغ

پري ندارد اي صنم بروشني چنين جبين
بشر دهد ازیں پسر که به بود زحورعین

چني جبين	بروشني	ردي صنم	پري ندا
مفاعلان	مفاعلن	مفاعلن	مفاعلن

زحورعین	کهبهبود	ازي پسر	بشردهد
مفاعلان	مفاعلن	مفاعلن	مفاعلن

هزج مثمن اشتر

سرومن دمي بنشین خانهرا گلستان کن
یکدوجام مي درکش دورنوش گردان کن

گلستاکن	خانرا	دمي بنشي	سرومن
مغاعیلن	فاعلن	مغاعیلن	رفاعلن

شکرداکن	دورنو	مهي درکش	یکدجا
مغاعیهلن	فاعلن	مغاعیلن	فاعلن

Scansion of Perfect Forms.

هزج مثمن اخرب

دل باز بجوش آمد جانان که مي آيد

بيمار بهوش آمد درمان که مي آيد

کهمي‌آيد	جانان	بجوشامد	دل‌باز
مفاعيلن	مفعول	مفاعيلن	مفعول

کهمي‌آيد	درمان	بهوشامد	بيمار
مفاعيلن	مفعول	مفاعيلن	مفعول

هزج مثمن اخرب مكفوف مقصور

تا چند مرا در غم او پند توان گفت

چيزي که بجايي نرسد چند توان گفت

تواگفت	مرادرغم	م‌اوپند	تلچند
مفاعيل	مفاعيل	مفاعيل	مفعول

تواكفت	ريسدچند	بجايي‌ن	چيزي‌که
مفاعيل	مفاعيل	مفاعيل	مفعول

Scansion of Perfect Forms.

هزج مثمن اخرب مكفوف محذوف

اي شيخ مرا راه خرابات نمودي
ميخواست دلم باده كرامات نمودي

نمودي	خرابات	مراراه	اي شيخ
فعول	مفاعيل	مفاعيل	مفعول

نمودي	كرامات	دلم باد	ميخاس
فعول	مفاعيل	مفاعيل	مفعول

هزج مثمن مكفوف مقصور

زهي حسن وزهي روي و زهي نور و زهي نار
زهي خط و زهي خال و زهي مور و زهي مار

زهي نار	زهي نور	زهي روي	زهي حسن
مفاعيل	مفاعيل	مفاعيل	مفاعيل

زهي مار	زهي مور	زهي خال	زهي خط
مفاعيل	مفاعيل	مفاعيل	مفاعيل

Scansion of Perfect Forms.

هزج مثمن مكفوف محذوف

مرا عشق دو تا كرد بهنگام جواني
چرا باز بيرسي توز حالم چو بداني

جواني	بهنگام	دتاكرد	مراعشق
فعول	مفاعيل	مفاعيل	مفاعيل

بداني	زحالبچ	بيرسيت	چراباز
فعولن	مفاعيل	مفاعيل	مفاعيل

هزج مسدس مقصور

يكى از درد مندان تو ماببيم
بيا تا درد مند يها نبا ببيم

تاماببيم	دمنداني	يكي ازدر
مفاعيل	مفاعيلن	مفاعيلن

نبابيم	دمنديها	بياتادر
مفاعيل	مفاعيل	مفاعيل

Scansion of Perfect Forms.

هزج مسدس محذوف

دلا در عشق رنج‌ما كشيدي
كرم كردي و زحمتها كشيدي

كشيدي	قدانجى‌ما	دلادرعش
فعولن	مفاعيلن	مفاعي‌بلن

كشيدي	وزحمتها	كرم كردي
فعولن	مفاعيلن	مفاعيلن

هزج مسدس مكفوف متقصور

بتاخيز و بيارآن مى خوشبوي
كه هبرنك بود با كل خود روي

ى‌خشبوي	بيارام	بتاخير
مفاعيل	مفاعيل	مفاعيل

ل‌خدروي	بودباك	كهبرنك
مفاعيل	مفاعيل	مفاعيل

6

Scansion of Perfect Forms.

هزج مسدس مكفوف محذوف

دل آزارو جفاكار نكاري

چز آزار دلم كار نداري

نشكاري	جفاكار	دلازار
فعولن	مفاعيل	مفاعيل

نداري	دلم كار	جزازار
فعولن	مفاعيل	مفاعيل

هزج مسدس اخرب مقبوض

اي از مزهٔ تور خنه درجانها

وي درد توكيبياي درمانها

ندرجاها	زبي ترخ	اي ازم
مفاعيلن	مفاعلن	مفعول

ي درماها	تكيبيا	وي درد
مفاعيلن	مفاعلن	مفعول

Scansion of Perfect Forms.

هزج مسدس اخرب مقبوض مقصور

گفتي لب من چو انگبين است

خود کو مزه در کجاي اين است

گفتيل	بمن چوان	گبينست
مفعول	مفاعلن	مفاعيل

خدکوم	زدرکجا	يي اينست
مفعول	مفاعلن	مفاعيل

هزج مسدس اخرب مقبوض محذوف

تا عشق پري رخان گزيدم

از روي خوشي نشان نديدم

تاعشق	پري رخا	گزيدم
مفعول	مفاعلن	فعولن

ازروي	خشي نشا	نديدم
مفعول	مفاعلن	فعولن

Scansion of Perfect Forms.

هزج مسدس اخرب مكفوف مجذوف

از دست و زبان. که برآید

گر عهده شکرش بدرآید

براید	زبانی که	از دست
فعولن	مفاعيل	مفعول

درايد	يشكرش ب	گرعهد
فعولن	مفاعيل	مفعول

هزج مسدس اشتر

باغ را مژده بهار آمد

نكهت نافه تتار آمد

بهارامد	مژدبی	باغرا
مفاعيلن	فاعلن	فاعلن

تتارامد	نافیي	نکهتي
مفاعيلن	فاعلن	فاعلن

PROSODY.

Scansion of Perfect Forms.

هزج مسدس اخرب اشتر مقصور

صد باره بیش اگر کشی زار

بر خیزم تا کشی دگر بلا

صدیارم	بیش گر	کشی زار
مفعولن	فاعلن	مفاعیل

برخیزم	تاکشی	دگر بلا
مفعولن	فاعلن	مفاعیل

رجز مثمن، مذال

یارب چه شد کان ترک ماترک مهربان کرده است

آسود کان وصل رار نجور هجران کرده است

یارب چه شد	کاترک ما	ترک محب	باکرد است
مستفعلن	مستفعلن	مستفعلن	مستفعلان

السودکا	نی وصل را	رنجور هم	راکرد است
مستفعلن	مستفعلن	مستفعلن	مستفعلان

Scansion of Perfect Forms.

رجز مثمن مطوي

مي شگفد گل بچمنهاز نسيم سحري
وہ چہ شود گرنغسي پهلوي ماباده خوري

مي شگفد گل بچين هازنسي مي سحري
مفتعلن   مفتعلن   مفتعلن   مفتعلن

وہ چہ شود   گرنغسي   پهلي ما   بادخري
مفتعلن   مفغعلن   مفتعلن   مفتعلن

رجز مثمن مطوي مخبون

باز خدنك شوق زد عشق در آب و خاك ما
نطع حريف مست شد دامن چاك چاك ما

باوخدن   گشوق زد   عشق درا   بخاك ما
مفتعلن   مفاعلن   مفاعلن   مفتعلن

نطع حري   فا مست شد   دامن چا   ك چاك ما
مفتعلن   مفاعلن   مفتعلن   مفتعلن

Scansion of Perfect Forms.

رجز مثمن مخبون مطوي

فغان كنان هرسحري بكويتو مي گذرم
چونيست ره سوي توام ببام و در مي نگرام

فغاكنا   هرسحري   بكوي‌تو   مي گذرم
مفاعلن   مفتعلن   مفاعلن   مفتعلن

چ نيس ره   سوي‌تام   ببام‌در   مي‌نكرم
مفاعلن   مفتعلن   مفاعلن   مفتعلن

رجز مسدس مطوي

نيست مرا جز تو نگارا دگري
مي نكني هيچ بكارم نظري

نيس‌مرا   جرتنگا   راد‌گري
مفتعلن   مفتعلن   مفتعلن

مي‌نكني   هيچ‌بكا   رم‌نظري
مفتعلن   مفتعلن   مفتعلن

Scansion of Perfect Forms.

رجز مسدس مخبون

كنون كه گردد. از بهار خوش هوا

فزون شود بهر دل اندرون هوا

كنون كگر   دد زبها •   رخش هوا

مفاعلن   مفاعلن   مفاعلن

فزو شود   بهر دلن   دروهوا

مفاعلن   مفاعلن   مفاعلن

ومل مثمن مسبع

تابكي گريم بزاري همچو ابرنو بهاران

ا: سراند وه وحسرت در فراق گلعذاران

تابكي گر   يم بزاري   همچ ابري   نوبهاران

فاعلاتن   فاعلاتن   فاعلاتن   فاعليان

ازسري ان   دوه حسرت   در فراقي   نوبهاران

فاعلاتن   فاعلاتن   فاعلاتن   فاعليان

Scansion of Perfect Forms.

رمل مثمن مخبون

شکرترا شد اگر چه سپه مور مرتب
مگسی نیز نخواهم که کند سایه بران لب

شکرترا شدَگرچی سپهیمو رمرتب
فعلاتن فعلاتن فعلاتن فعلاتن

مگسینی زنخاهم کهکندسا ی برالب
فعلاتن فعلاتن فعلاتن فعلاتن

رمل مثمن مقصور

هرکجا بینم مهی با عاشق خود مهربان
افتد از بی مهری ماه خودم آتش بجان

هرکجابی نممهیبا عاشقیخد مهربا
فاعلاتن فاعلاتن فاعلاتن فاعلات

افتدزبی مهربیما هیخدماا تش بجان
فاعلاتن فاعلاتن فاعلاتن فاعلات

Scansion of Perfect Forms.

رمل مثمن محذوف

هر كرا بينم سخن با اوز هرجا ميكنم
تاكند ذكر تو صد تقريب پيدا ميكنم

هركرابي نم سخن با اوزهرجا ميكنم
فاعلاتن فاعلاتن فاعلاتن فاعلن

تاكندذك ريت صد تق ريب پيدا ميكنم
فاعلاتن فاعلاتن فاعلاتن فاعلن

وسل بثمن مشكول

قدزي بخند و ازرخ قمري نباي مارا
سختي بكوي وازلب شكري نباي مارا

قدر يب نخنداز رخ قمرين ماي مارا
فعلات فاعلاتن فعلات فاعلاتن

سخنيب كوي ازلب شكرين ماي مارا
فعلات فاعلاتن فعلات فاعلاتن

Scansion of Perfect Forms.

رمل مثمن مشكول مسبغ

منم و خیال بازي شب ُو روز با جوانان
زخط خوش تو با خود رقم خیال خوانان

منم‌وخ یال‌بازي شب‌روز باجوانان
فعلات فاعلاتن فعلات فاعلیان

زخطبخ شیت‌باخد رقبیخ یال‌خانان
فعلات فاعلاتن فعلات فاعلایان

رمل مثمن مخبون مسبغ

روزکار یست که در خاطرم آشوب فلان است
روزکارم چو سرزلف پریشانش ازان است

روزکاري سكه‌درخا طرماشو بغلانست
فاعلاتن فعلاتن فعلاتن فعلیان

روزکارم چسري‌زل فپریشا نشزانست
فاعلاتن فعلاتن فعلاتن فعلیان

Scansion of Perfect Forms.

رمل مثمن مخبون مقصور

چارہ هجر تو سازم بو صال د ثران
آہ تا چند کشم بي تو محال د کران

دکران   بوصالي   رتسازم   چاریہ هج
نعلات   نعلاتن   نعلاتن   فاعلاتن

دکران   تهحالي   دکشمبي   اہتاچن
نعلات   نعلاتن   نعلاتن   فاعلاتن

رمل مثمن مخبون محذوف

گرچه مقصود بلابي دل و دين است مرا
هيچ غم نيست که مقصود هيين است مرا

تہرا   دل دينس   دبلابي   گرچہ مقصو
نعلن   نعلاتن   نعلاتن   فاعلاتن

تہرا   دهينس   سکمہ مقصو   هيبچ غم ني
نعلن   نعلاتن   نعلاتن   فاعلاتن

Scansion of Perfect Forms.

رمل مثمن مخبون مقطوع

ساخت برک طرب و عيش مهيا نرگس
تاكشد بادف ونی ساغرصهبا نرگس

نرگس	شهبیا	طربوعی	ساخ برگبی
فعلن	فعلاتن	فعلاتن	فاعلاتن

نرگس	غرصهبا	دفنی سا	تاکشدبا
فعلن	فعلاتن	فعلاتن	فاعلاتن

رمل مثمن مخبون مقطوع مسبغ

پیش ازین ترچه ببویت رخ گل میدیدیم
چون گل روی تو دیدیم از و واچندیم

دیدیم	رخ گلمی	چهببویت	پیش زی گر
فعلان	فعلاتن	فعلاتن	فاعلاتن

چیدیم	م ازروا	یتدید	چوگلیرو
فعلان	فعلاتن	فعلاتن	فاعلاتن

Scansion of Perfect Forms.

رمل مسدس مقصور

تالب او ديد سيغي در شراب

از مثلث مي نبايد اجتناب

درشراب	ديدسيغي	تالبـاو
فاعلان	فاعلاتن	فاعلاتن

اجتناب	مينبايد	ازمثلث
فاعلات	فاعلاتن	فاعلاتن

رمل مسدس محذوف

گفت زاهد از بهشتم ده خبر

گفتمش زنهار نام ده مبر

دهخبر	ازبهشتم	گفتزاهد
فاعلن	فاعلاتن	فاعلاتن

دهمبر	هارنامي	گفتمش‌زن
فاعلن	فاعلاتن	فاعلاتن

Scansion of Perfect Forms.

رمل مسدس مخبون مقصور

شکرین لعل تو کان نبک است

ٱرچه شِکرنه مکان نبک است

نبکست	لتکانی	شککریلع
فعلات	فعلاتن	فاعلاتن

نبکست	نهکانی	ٱرچهشککر
فعلان	فعلاتن	فاعلاتن

رمل مسدس مخبون محذوف

ٱرسخن زان لب چون نوش شود

پستهرا خنده فراموش شود

ششود	لبچونو	ٱزسخنزا
فعلن	فعلاتن	فاعلاتن

ششود	دفرامو	پستراخن
فعلن	فعلاتن	فاعلاتن

Scansion of Perfect Forms.

رمل مسدس مخبون مقطوع

مردمي نرگس او ميد اند
جادويي غمزه او ميخوانند

مردمي نر	ثس اومي	دانند
فاعلاتن	فعلاتن	فعلن

جادبي غم	زي اومي	خاند
فاعلاتن	فعلاتن	فعلن

رمل مسدس مخبون مقطوع مسبغ

اي كه رويي تو حيات جان است
ديده جايت شد و جابي آنست

اي كرويي	تحياتي	جانست
فاعلاتن	فعلاتن	فعلان

ديدجايت	شدجابي	انست
فاعلاتن	فعلاتن	فعلان

Scansion of Perfect Forms.

منسرح مثمن مطوي موقوف

انکه دلم صید اوست میر شکار من است

دست بخونم نگار کرده نگار من است

ااکدلم	صیداوس	میرشکا	ری‌منست
مفتعلن	فاعلات	مفتعلن	فاعلات

دست‌بخو	نم‌نگار	کردنگا	ری‌منست
مفتعلن	فاعلات	مفتعلن	فاعلات

منسرح مثمن مطوي مكسوف

اي زرخت روشني خانه چشم مرا

چشم و چراغ من است خواجه هردو سرا

اي‌زرخت	روشني	حاني‌چش	مي‌مرا
مفتعلن	فاعلن	مفتعلن	فاعلن

چشم‌چرا	غي‌منس	خاجی	دوسرا
مفتعبلن	فاعلن	مفتعلن	فاعلن

Scansion of Perfect Forms.

رجز مسدس مخبون

كنون كه گردد. از بهار خوش هوا
فزون شود بهر دل اندرون هوا

كنوككر   ددزبها •   رخش هوا
مفاعلن   مفاعلن   مفاعلن

فزوشود   بهردلن   دروهوا
مفاعلن   مفاعلن   مفاعلن

رمل مثمن مسبع

تابكي گريم بزاري همچو ابرنو بهاران
اِ سراند وه وحسرت در فراق گلعذاران

تابكى گر   يم بزارى   همچ ابرى   نوبهاران
فاعلاتن   فاعلاتن   فاعلاتن   فاعليان

ازسري ان   دوه حسرت   در فراقي   نوبهاران
فاعلاتن   فاعلاتن   فاعلاتن   فاعليان

Scansion of Perfect Forms.

رمل مثمن مخبون

شكرترا شد اگر چه سپه مور مرتب
مگسی نیز نخواهم که کند سایه بران لب

شكرترا   شدَ ترچِی   سپهیمو   ومرتب
فعلاتن   فعلاتن   فعلاتن   فعلاتن

مگسینی   زتخاهم   کهکندسا   یبرالب
فعلاتن   فعلاتن   فعلاتن   فعلاتن

رمل مثمن مقصور

هرکجا بینم مهی با عاشق خود مهربان
افتد از بی مهری ماه خودم آتش بجان

هرکجابی   نممهیبا   عاشقیخد   مهربا
فاعلاتن   فاعلاتن   فاعلاتن   فاعلات

افتدزبی   مهربیما   هیخدماا   تشبجان
فاعلاتن   فاعلاتن   فاعلاتن   فاعلات

Scansion of Perfect Forms.

مضارع مثمن اخرب

سبغي كدا از ازان شد در شهر آن پريرو
تا روز هاي دوران آيد بجانب او

سبعيك داازاشد درشهر الپريرو
مفعول فاعلاتن مفعول فاعلاتن

تاروز هاي‌دورا ايدب جانبي‌او
مفعول فاعلاتن مفعول فاعلاتن

مضارع مثمن اخرب مسبغ

ثرا عتقاد آن مه با ماكم وز يباد است
ماييم و مهر رويش مقصود اعتقاد است

ثراعت قاداامه باماك موزيادست
مفعول فاعلاتن مفعول فاعليان

ماييم مهررويش مقصود اعتقادست
مفعول فاعلاتن مفعول فاعليان

Scansion of Perfect Forms.

مضارع مثمن اخرب مكفوف

دل بي رخ تو جو هرجان رانمي شناسد
جان بي لب تو ثو هركان رانمي شناسد

مي‌شناسد	رجاران	خيث‌جوه	دل‌بير
فاعلاتن	مفاعيل	فاعلات	مفعول

مي‌شناسد	ركاران	بيت‌ثوه	جابيل
فاعلاتن	مفاعيل	فاعلات	مفعول

مضارع مثمن اخرب مكفوف مقصور

بازم هواي آن لب ميكون كرفته است
معلوم ميشود كه مرا خون كرفته است

رفتاست	يبيگوك	واي‌ال	بازمه
فاعلات	مفاعيل	فاعلات	مفعول

رفتاست	مراخوكه	ميشودكه	معلوم
فاعلات	مفاعيل	فاعلات	مفعول

Scansion of Perfect Forms.

مضارع مثمن اخرب مكفوف محذوف

سيغبي پري وشي كة تو ديوانه ازو
خواهي مسخر تو شود جز دعا مگو

بي ازو	تديوان	ري وشيك	سيغيپ
فاعلن	مفاعيل	فاعلات	مفعول

عامثو	شودجرد	سخخريث	خاهيم
فاعلن	مفاعيل	فاعلات	مفعول

مضارع مثمن مكفوف مقصور

كران طره هست مشك بهاچون نداد بوي
ورآك چهره هست ماه چرا دركشيد روي

دادبوي	بهاچون	هست مشك	گراطر
فاعلات	مفاعيل	فاعلات	مفاعيل

شبدروي	چرادرك	هست ماه	وراچهر
فاعلات	مفاعيل	فاعلات	مفاعيل

Scansion of Perfect Forms.

رمل مثمن مخبون مقطوع

ساخت برک طرب و عيش مهيا نرگس

تا كشد بادف و ني سا غرصهبا نرگس

نرگس	شهبيا	طربوعي	ساخبرگني
فعلن	فعلاتن	فعلاتن	فاعلاتن

نرگس	غرصهبا	دفنيسا	تاكشدبا
فعلن	فعلاتن	فعلاتن	فاعلاتن

رمل مثمن مخبون مقطوع مسبغ

پيش ازين ترچه ببويت رخ گل ميديديم

چون گل روي تو ديديم از و واچنديم

ديديم	رخ گلمي	چهببويت	پيش زي گر
فعلان	فعلاتن	فعلاتن	فاعلاتن

چيديم	مازووا	يتدنيد	چوگليرو
فعلان	فعلاتن	فعلاتن	فاعلاتن

Scansion of Perfect Forms.

رمل مسدس مقصور

تالب او دید سیغی در شراب
از مثلث می نهاید اجتناب

درشراب	دیدسیغی	تالباو
فاعلان	فاعلاتن	فاعلاتن

اجتناب	مینهاید	ازمثلث
فاعلات	فاعلاتن	فاعلاتن

رمل مسدس محذوف

گفت زاهد از بهشتم یده خبر
گفتمش زنهار نام ده مبر

دهخبر	ازبهشتم	گفتزاهد
فاعلن	فاعلاتن	فاعلاتن

دهمبر	هارنامی	کغتمش زن
فاعلن	فاعلاتن	فاعلاتن

Scansion of Perfect Forms.

رمل مسدس مخبون مقصور

شكرين لعل تو كان نبك است

گرچه شكرنه مكان نبك است

نبكست	لت‌كاني	شكَّكري‌لع
فعلات	فعلاتن	فاعلاتن

نبكست	نهكاني	گرچهشككر
فعلان	فعلاتن	فاعلاتن

رمل مسدس مخبون محذوف

گرسخن زان لب چون نوش شود

بستهرا خنده فراموش شود

ششود	لب‌چونو	گرسخن‌زا
فعلن	فعلاتن	فاعلاتن

ششود	دفرامو	بست‌راخن
فعلن	فعلاتن	فاعلاتن

Scansion of Perfect Forms.

رمل مسدس مخبون مقطوع

مردمي نرگس او ميد اند
جادويي غمزه او ميخواند

داند	ثس او مي	مردمي نر
فعلن	فعلاتن	فاعلاتن

خاند	زي او مي	جادي غم
فعلن	فعلاتن	فاعلاتن

رمل مسدس مخبون مقطوع مسبغ

اي كه رويي تو حيات جان است
ديده جايت شد و جابي آنست

جانست	تحياتي	اي كروبي
فعلان	فعلاتن	فاعلاتن

انست	شدجايي	ديدجايت
فعلان	فعلاتن	فاعلاتن

6

Scansion of Perfect Forms.

منسرح مثمن مطوي موقوف

انكه دلم صيد اوست مير شكار من است
دست بخونم نگار كرده نگار من است

اكدلم صيداوس ميرشكا ري‌منست

مفتعلن فاعلات مفتعلن فاعلات

دست‌بخو نم‌نگار كردنگا ري‌منست

مفتعلن فاعلات مفتعلن فاعلات

منسرح مثمن مطوي مكسوف

اي زرخت روشني خانه چشم مرا
چشم و چراغ من است خواجه هردو سرا

اي‌زرخت روشني حاني‌چش مي‌مرا

مفتعلن فاعلن مفتعلن فاعلن

چشم‌چرا غي‌منس خاجي دوسرا

مفتعلن فاعلن مفتعلن فاعلن

Scansion of Perfect Forms.

مغسرح مثمن مطوي مجدوع

من نشنيدم كه خط بر آب نويسند
آيت خوبي بر آنتاب نويسند

سند	رابنوي	دم كخطب	من نشني
فاع	مفتعلن	فاعلات	مفتعلن

سند	تابنوي	بى يراف	ايتخو
فاع	مفتعلن	فاعلات	مفتعلن

منسرح مثمن مطوي منحور

چون غم هجران اونداشت نهايت
عاقبت اندوه عشق كرد سرابت

يت	داشنها	ران اون	چوغم هج
نع	متعلن	فاعلات	مفتعلن

يت	كردسرا	دوه عشق	عاقبتن
نع	مفتعلن	فاعلات	مفتعلى

Scansion of Perfect Forms.

منسرح مسدس مطوي

شاه جهان باد تازمانه بود
كز كرمش خلق شاد مانه بود

مانبود	بادتاز	شاهجها
مفتعلن	فاعلات	مفتعلن

مانبود	خلقشاد	كزكرمش
مفتعلن	فاعلات	مفتعلن

منسرح مسدس مطوي مقطوع

بسكه بـوبت اسير شد جانم
گربگذد اري گربخت نتوانم

شدجانم	يثاسير	بسكهبو
مغولن	فاعلات	مفتعلن

نتوالم	ريگربخ	كربگذا
مفتعلن	فاعلات	مفتعلن

Scansion of Perfect Forms.

مضارع مثمن اخرب

سبغني شدا از ازان شد در شهر آن پريرو

تا روز هاي دوران آيد بجانب او

الپريرو	در شهر	د از ازان شد	سبعيك
فاعلاتن	مفعول	فاعلاتن	مفعول

حانبي او	الايدب	هاي دورا	تاروز
فاعلاتن	مفعول	فاعلاتن	مفعول

مضارع مثمن اخرب مسبغ

ثرا عتقاد آن مه با ماكم وز ياد است

ماييم و مهر رويش مقصود اعتقاد است

موز يادست	با ماک	قاد امه	ثراعت
فاعليان	مفعول	فاعلاتن	مفعول

اعتقادست	مقصود	مهر رويش	ماييم
فاعليان	مفعول	فاعلاتن	مفعول

Scansion of Perfect Forms.

مضارع مثمن اخرب مكفوف

دل بي رخ تو جو هرجان رائمي شناسد
جان بي لب تو ثو هركان رائمي شناسد

مي شناسد	رجاران	خيث جوه	دل بير
فاعلاتن	مفاعيل	فاعلات	مفعول

مي شناسد	ركاران	بيت گوه	جابيل
فاعلاتن	مفاعيل	فاعلات	مفعول

مضارع مثمن اخرب مكفوف مقصور

بازم هواي آن لب ميگون كرفته است
معلوم ميشود كه مرا خون كرفته است

رفت است	ييگوك	واي ال	بازمه
فاعلات	مفاعيل	فاعلات	مفعول

رفت است	مراخوكه	ميشود كه	معلوم
فاعلات	مفاعيل	فاعلات	مفعول

Scansion of Perfect Forms.

مضارع مثمن اخرب مكفوف محذوف

سیغبی پری وشی کة تو دیوانه ازو
خواهی مسخر تو شود جز دعا مگو

یی ازو	تدیوان	ری وشیک	سیغیپ
فاعلن	مفاعیل	فاعلات	مفعول

عامثو	شودجرد	سخریت	خاهیم
فاعلن	مفاعیل	فاعلات	مفعول

مضارع مثمن مكفوف مقصور

کران طره هست مشک بهاچون نداد بوی
ورآك چهره هست ماه چرا درکشید روی

دادبوی	بهاچون	هستمشک	گراطرر
فاعلات	مفاعیل	فاعلات	مفاعیل

شیدروی	چرادرک	هستماه	وراچهر
فاعلات	مفاعیل	فاعلات	مفاعیل

PROSODY.

Scansion of Perfect Forms.

مضارع مسدس اخرب مكفوف

اي ناز نين كه ماه مني امشب

رحمى بكن چو شاه مني امشب

اي‌ناز   نی‌كه‌ماه   مني‌امشب

مفعول   فاعلات   مفاعيلن

رحیيب كن‌چشاه   مني‌امشب

مفعول   فاعلات   مفاعيلن

مقتضب مثمن مطوي

بالبت چه مى طلبم باده نزد جان چه بود

بارخت چه مه نگرم بنده پيش خان چه بود

بالبتچ   ميطلبم   بادنزد   جاچه‌بود

فاعلات   مفتعلن   فاعلات   مفتعلن

بارختچ   مننگرم   بندپيش   خاچه‌بود

فاعلات   مفتعلن   فاعلات   مفتعلن

Scansion of Perfect Forms.

مقتضب مثمن مطوي مقطوع

وقترا غنیمت دان آنقدر که بَتوانی
حاصل از حیات ای جان یکدم است تادانی

وقتراغ	نیبت‌دا	اقدرک	بتوانی
فاعلات	مفعولن	فاعلات	مفعولن

حاصلزح	یاتی‌جا	یکدمست	تادانی
فاعلات	مفعولن	فاعلات	مفعولن

مجتث مثمن مخبون

زدور نیست میسر نظر بروی تو مارا
چه دولت است تعالی الله ازقد توقبارا

زدورنی	سبیسر	نظربرو	یتبارا
مفاعلن	فعلاتن	مفاعلن	فعلاتن

چدولتس	تتعالل	لهزقدی	تقبارا
مفاعلن	فعلاتن	مفاعلن	فعلاتن

Scansion of Perfect Forms.

مجتث مثمن مخبون مسبغ

دلم كه سوخت زعشقت چراغ جان من است آن

غبار كز تو رسد نور ديد كان من انست آن

نهنستان	چراغجا	خزعشقت	دلمكسو
يفعليان	مفاعلن	فعلاتن	مفاعلن

نهنستان	رديدكا	ترسدنو	غباركز
فعليان	مفاعلن	فعلاتن	مفاعلن

مجتث مثمن مخبون مقصور

زبسكه درد تو بر جان نا توان من است

هلاك من طلبد هركه مهربان من است

نهنست	نناتوا	دتبرجا	زبسكدر
فعلات	مفاعلن	فعلاتن	مفاعلن

نهنست	كهربا	طلبدهر	هلاكمن
فعلات	مفاعلن	فعلاتن	مفاعلن

Scansion of Perfect Forms.

مجتث مثمن مخبون محذوف

شفا چو در قدم تست مبتلاي ترا

برون خرام که دردي مباد پاي ترا

شفاچدر قدميتس تبتلا يترا

مفاعلن فعلاتن مفاعلن فعلن

بروخرا مكدردي مبادپا يترا

مفاعلن فعلاتن مفاعلن فعلن

مجتث مثمن مخبون مقطوع

اگر چه يار مرا نيست رسم دلد اري

بدين خوشم که ندارد بد يكري ياري

اگرچيا رمرانی سرسم دل داري

مفاعلن فعلاتن مفاعلن فعلن

بديخشم كندارد بديكري ياري

مفاعلن فعلاتن مفاعلن فعلن

Scansion of Perfect Forms.

مجتث مثمن مخبون مقطوع مسبغ

چو ڳویم از سرمستي لبت مي ناب است

مرنج از سخن ما كه عالم آب است

نابست	لبتـميي	سرمستي	چڳوييز
فعلان	مفاعلن	فعلاتن	مفاعلن

البست	كعالـي	سخني‌ما	مرنج‌از
فعلان	مفاعلن	فعلاتن	مفاعلن

سريع مطوي موقوف

دل كه زخوبان هيه غم ديده است

بيشتر از عمر ستم ديده است

ديداست	باهم‌غم	دل‌كزخو
فاعلات	مفتعلن	مفتعلن

ديداست	عمرستم	بيشترز
فاعلاث	مفعلن	مفتعلن

Scansion of Perfect Forms.

سريع مطوي مكسوف

كي بود آندم كه ببزم وفا

مي بدل ما كشد آن دلربا

مي وفا	دم كبنز	كي بودا
فاعلن	مفتعلن	مفتعلن

دلربا	ماكشدا	مي بدلي
فاعلن	مفتعلن	مفتعلن

جديد مخبون

چوقدت كرچه صنو بر كشد سري

نبود چون قد سروت صنو بري

كشد سري	چصنوبر	چقدت ثر
مفاعلن	فعلاتن	فعلاتن

صنوبري	قد سروت	نبود چو
مفاعلن	فعلاتن	فعلاتن

Scansion of Perfect Forms.

قريب مكفوف

خداوند جهان بخش شاه عادل
خداوند چهابخش شاهءعادل
شهنشاه جوان بخت زاد كامل

فاعلاتن	مغاعيل	مغاعيل

زادكامل	جوابخت	شهنشاه
فاعلاتن	مغاعيل	مفاعيل

قريب اخرب مكفوف

تاطبع رهي برقرار باشد
مداح در شهريار باشد

رارباشد	رهيبرق	تاطبع
فاعلاتن	مغاعيل	مفعول

يارباشد	دريشهر	مداح
فاعلاتن	مغاعيل	مفعول

Scansion of Perfect Forms.

خفيف مخبون

اي صبا بوسه زن زمن در اورا

ور نرنجد لب چو شكر اورا

دراورا	سزن زمن	اي‌صبابو
فعلاتن	مفاعلن	فاعلاتن

كراورا	لبی‌چشک	ورنرنجد
فعلاتن	مفاعلن	فاعلاتن

خفيف مخبون مقصور

ماه رويا بخون من مشتاب

كشتن عاشقان كه ديد صواب

مشتاب	بخون‌من	ماه‌رويا
فعلات	مفاعلن	فاعلاتن

دصواب	شفاكدي	كشتن‌عا
نعلات	مفاعلن	فاعلاتن

PROSODY.

Scansion of Perfect Forms.

خفيف مخبون محذوف

گفتمش بي تو چيست چاره ما

رفت در قهر و گفت مرگ و بلا

گفتمش‌بي   تچیس‌چا   ریبا

فاعلاتن   مفاعلن   فعلن

رفت‌درقه   رگفت‌مر   گبلا

فاعلاتن   مفاعلن   فعلن

خفيف مخبون مقطوع

با توكي درد ما توان گفتن

اين سخن را كجا توان گفتن

باتكي‌در   دماتوا   گفتن

فاعلاتن   مفاعلن   فعلن

اي‌سخن‌را   كجاتوا   گفتن

فاعلاتن   مفاعلن   فعلن

Scansion of Perfect Forms.

خفيف مخبون مصطوع مسبغ

از طبايع هر انچه موجود است
آد مي زان ميانه مقصود است

ازطبابع	هرنچمو	جودست
فاعلاتن	مفاعلن	فعلان

الامي‌زا	ميانبق	صودست
فاعلاتن	مفاعلن	فعلان

مشاكل مكفوف مقصور

يار غم شده ام در شب ديجور
زان سبب كه نشد درد محب دور

يارغمش	دام‌درش	بديجور
فاعلات	مفاعيل	مفاعيل

زاسببكه	نشددرد	محبدور
فاعلات	مفاعيل	مفاعيل

Scansion of Perfect Forms.

متقارب مثمن مقصور

مراكشت آن مه چو هجران نبود

زمرگم خبر بود و زيينم نبود

مراكش تاامه چهجرا نبود

فعولن فعولن فعولن فعولن

زمرگم خبربو دزينم نبود

فعولن فعولن فعولن فعول

متقارب مثمن محذوف

چوآيم بكويت مكن عيب من

كه بي اختيارم درين آمدن

چأايم بكويت مكنعي بهن

فعولن فعولن فعولن فعل

كنبياخ تيارم درياا مدن

فعولن فعولن فعولن فعل

Scansion of Perfect Forms.

متقارب مثمن اثلم

آشوب جاني شوخ جهاني
بي اعتقادي نا مهرباني

جهاني	شوخي	بجاني	االشو
فعولن	فعلن	فعولن	فعلن

ربانى	نامه	تقادي	بي‌اع
فعولن	فعلن	فعولن	فعلن

متقارب مثمن مقبوض اثلم

گرم بخوانی ورم براني
دل حزين را بجاي جاني

راني	ورنب	خاني	گروب
فعلن	فعول	فعلن	فعول

جاني	بجاي	زيرا	دليح
فعلن	فعول	فعلن	فعول

Scansion of Perfect Forms.

متدارك مثمن مخبون

چو رخت نبود گل باغ ارم
چو قدت نبود قد سرو چمن

چرخت   نبود   گل با   غارم
فعلن   نِعلن   فعلن   فعلن

چقدت   نبود   قدسر   وچمن
فعلن   فعلن   فعلن   فعلن

متدارك مثمن مقطوع

هردم پیشت دارم زاري
كزغم تاكي زارم داري

هردم   پییشت   دارم   زاري
فعلن   فعلن   فعلن   فعلن

كزغم   تاكي   زارم   داري
فعلن   فعلن   فعلن   فعلن

Scansion of Perfect Forms.

متدارک مثمن مخبون مقطوع

سنبل سیه برسمن مزن
لشکر حبش برختن مزن

سنبلي سیه برسمں مزن
فاعلن فعل فاعلن فعل

لشكري حبش برختن مزن
فاعلن فعل فاعلن فعل

Forms of the Ru-ba-ie:

اوزان رباعي از شجرهٔ اخرم

هجرانت خون‌ابسي مرا در دل كرد
واند وهت در سينه من منزل كرد
ديگر تا كي فزاييم محنت و غم
كس هركز اين سخن بابيدل كرد

كرد	مراد ردل	خوبسي	هجرانت
فاع	مفاعيلن	فاعلن	مفعولن

كرد	يبن‌منزل	درسين	وندوهت
فاع	مفاعيلن	مفعول	مفعولن

تغم	بيم محن	كي فزا	ديكرتا
فعل	مفاعيل	فاعلن	مفعولن

كرد	بابيدل	اي سخن	كس هركز
فاع	مفعولن	فاعلن	مفعولن

يار آمد يار آمد يار آمد هي
بنشيني بيخبر بديبيسان تاكبي

Forms of the Ru-ba-ie.

يكساعت ازان ماه جبين دورمباش

تايابي! از جام لب لعلش مي

هي	يارامد	يارامد	يارامد
فع	مفعولن	مفعولن	مفعولن

كي	بدي‌سانا	ببيخبر	بنشيني
فع	مفاعيلن	فاعلن	مفعولن

مباش	دور	جبي‌دور	ازماه	يكساعت
فعول	عفاعيل	مفاعيل	مفعولن

مى	لعلش	لبي‌لعلش	ازجام	تايابي
فع	مفاعيلن	مفعول	مفعولن

جان دادم درراه وفايي صنمي

دل كردم قربانش بي بيش و كمي

از دستم كار كرنيايد چه غم است

دردیده‌ودل‌بس‌است‌سوزي ونمي

Forms of the Ru-ba-ie

جاد ادم   در راه   وفابی ص   نبي

مفعولن   مفعول   مفاعيل   فعل

دل کردم   قربانش   ببيبي   شکبي

مفعولن   مفعولن   فعلن   فعلن

از دستم   کارگر   نيايدچه   غبست

مفعولن   فاعلن   مفاعيل   فعول

درديد   رادل بسس   تسوزيا   نبن

مفعول   مفاعلن   مفاعيل   فعل

اوزان رباعي از شجرہ اخرب

اي عشق ترا چو من هزاران طالب

ديدار ترا يوسف مصري راغب

از هجر تو جانم را صد محنت و غم

آن به که نگردي تو از من غايب

اي عشق   ترا چبن   هزار اطا   لب

مفعول   مفاعلن   مفاعيلن   فع

Forms of the Ru-ba-ie.

عجب   قیصری‌را   ترایوس   دیدار
فع   مفاعیلن   مفاعیل   مفعول

تغم   صدمحن   تجانم‌را   ازهجر
فعل   مفعولن   مفاعیلن   مفعول

یب   ازمن‌غا   نگردی‌تو   ایه‌که
فع   مفعولن   مفاعیلن   مفعول

درپیش تو آوردم دل‌را به نیاز
دست من و زلف تو و امید دراز
درعالم پیش از من درمنده چونیست
آن به که نوازیم توای بنده نواز

نیاز   دل‌راب   تاوردم   درپیش
فعول   مفعول   مفاعیلن   مفعول

دراز   امید   نزلغی‌ت   دستیم
فعول   مفاعیل   مفاعیل   مفعول

Forms of the Ru-ba-ic.

درعالم بیشترمن درمند چنیس

مفعولن مفعولن مفعول فعول

اابه‌که نوازیم تای‌بند نواز

مفعول مفاعلن مفاعیل فعول

اي آنکه نبود يم زهجر انت زار
از کوه غمت دردل تنگم صد بار
خواهم که به پیش تو بکویم غم دل
چون چاره من بر تو نبود دشوار

اي‌ااکه نبودیم زهجرانت زار

مفعول مفاعلن مفاعیلن فاع

ازکوه غمت‌درد ل‌تنگم‌صد بار

مفعول مفاعیل مفاعیلن فاع

خاهم‌که بپیشی‌ت بکویم‌غ م‌دل

مفعول مفاعیل مفاعیل فعل

چوچار یمن‌برت نبودش وار

مفعولن مفاعیل مفعولن فاع

این غزل فیضي بچهار وزن خوانده مي شود

رمل مسدس مخبون محذوف	سریع مطوي مکسوف
فاعلاتن فعلاتن فعلن	مفتعلن مفتعلنٔ فاعلن
خفیف مخبون محذوف	رمل مسدس محذوف
فاعلاتن مفاعلن فعلن	فاعلاتن فاعلاتن فاعلن

حلقه کیسوي تو دام بلا	اي خم ابروي تو تیغ جفا
غمزه بد خوي تو تیر قضا	خنجر پهلوي تو تیغ اجل
کشته آهوي تو شیر خطا	بسته بازوي تو ترک ختن
در لب جادوي تو سر خدا	دررخ نیکوي تو نور ازل
دوخته هر سوي تو چشم هوا	تافته زانوي تو دست هوس
تشنه داروي تو بهر دوا	خسته هندوي تو فیضي

The foregoing Ode, by Sheikh Fizee, may be read in four different measures, as above described.

PART III.

———

RHYME.

PART III.

OF CA-FE-YEH,

OR

RHYME.

═══════════

Cá-fe-yeh قانيه is derived from تغو following another; and it is so called because it is used at the end of hemistichs or distichs, in different words, to complete the rhyme.

The conclusion of the *Cá-fe-yeh* is the last quiescent letter that occurs in a verse; and it is preceded by one or more accented, preceded by a quiescent, preceded by an accented letter, as in the words دِلبَرّي and پَروَري in the following distich:

دل زمن بستد بشوخي دلبري
دلبري شيرين لبي جان پروري

This rule is from Kháleel Ebn Ahmed, upon which Ukh-fusn remarks, that the *Cá-fe-yeh* includes the whole of the last word of the hemistich or distich.

Some again pretend that the final letter only is the *Cá-fe-yeh*; and although this is partly true, yet it is liable to objections, which will hereafter be produced.

The fact is, that the *Cá-fe-yeh* has determinate letters and accents, distinguished by appropriate names; and which are to be managed according to rule, in order to obviate irregularities and defects.

Explanation of the Letters forming the Cá-fe-yeh.

It is to be observed, that the *Re-wee* روي is the basis of the *Cá-fe-yeh* or rhyme, which cannot exist without it. *Re-wee* is the last quiescent letter of the rhyme, and other eight letters are united to it, four antecedent and four subsequent — the four antecedent are ردف 1 قيد 2 تاسيس 3 دخيل 4 and the four subsequent وصل 1 خروج 2 مزيد 3 يردنا 4

Of the Four Letters that precede Re-wee.

1. *Ridf* ردف implies either the letter ا quiescent, preceded by a letter accented with a *Futteh*; or و quiescent, preceded by a letter accented with a *Zum*; or ي quiescent, preceded by a letter accented with a *Kussir*; that is, whenever either of these three letters precedes the ر وي as in the following distichs of *Se-ná-ee*:

6

اي سنايي بقوت ايمَانْ
مدح حيدر بكوپس ازعُثمَانْ
آن علم دارو علم دار رَسُولْ
وين زفضل آفت سراي فُضُولْ
نشنيده زمصطفي تَأ و يْلْ
گشته مكشوف درد لش تَنْزِيْلْ

In the first distich, ن is روي and ا is ردف—in the second
distich, ل is روي and ر is روي and و is ردف—in the third distich,
and ي is ردف

But if after the ردف two quiescents occur, such as يافت and
گريخت and ريخت or پوست and دوست or تاقت in such case
some of the letters following the ردف are included therein, and are
called ردف زايد or redundant *Ridf*; but Nasser-ed-deen Tou-see,
in his treatise called معيار الاشعار includes these letters in the روي
and calls them روي مضاعف or redundant *Re-wee*.

In Persian the و and ي *Ridf* have both معروف or open, and
مجهول or sharp pronunciations. The first معروف or open, is
when *Zum* preceding و and the *Kussir* preceding ي is اشباع or
lengthened, as in the words دور and پور and ديد and چكيد
The second مجهول or sharp, is when the pronunciation is not
lengthened, as in the words زور and كور and بيد and اميد

Ancient authors have used them both together, as in the following distich of Se-ná-ee:

با و جودش اجل پر بر آمد
نیك آمد و لیك دبر آمد

The *Kussir* preceding the letter ي in the word پَرِبر is open, and in the word دبِر is sharp. In the following distich, - the *Zum* preceding و in عُوْر is open, and the *Zum* preceding و in گُوْر is sharp.

پیكر آب و شكل زشوقش عور
لعبت چشم و دل زكنهش كور

The letter ا softened into يردف or ي quiescent, preceded by a *Kussir*, when it immediately precedes the روي is not sounded open; as is exemplified in the following distich:

خلعتي كان تراست همچوجهیز
فستا ند بروز رستا خیز

2. *Ki-ed* قید is any quiescent, excepting the *Ridf* ا and و and ي and which are also called حروفـمد or letters capable of extension; in the following rhymes, the last letter is *Re-wee*, and the second letter is *Ki-ed*: thus درك and سرد—ابر and صبر—ختم and نشر and حشر—پشم and یشم—رزم and بزم مجد and وجد—شتم and حلم—دَ گر and فكر—نقل and عقل—نصر and قصر—امر and تبر—ننك and تنك—نبر and شبر And in *Cá-fe-yeh*, a difference in the letter *Ki-ed* is allowable; as in the following distich from the Gool-shun-ráz:

همه دانند که این کس در همه عمر
نکرد ه هیچ قصد گفتن شعر

Here in the word عمر the *Ki-ed* is م and in شعر it is ع In such
case it is proper to preserve the قرب مخرج or proximity of utterance ; as in the following distich of Sady :

چه مصر و چه شام و چه بر و چه بحر
همه روستایند و شیر از شهر

Here بحر and شهر have a proximity of utterance; the one from
the top, and the other from the bottom of the throat.

3. *Ta-sées* تاسیس or the quiescent ا preceding the روي between
which there occurs an accented letter called دخیل as in the
following rhymes : تساهل—سایل and مایل and باور and خاور and
تجاهل

It is allowable for the دخیل letter to be different, as in خاور
and چادر

And in rhyme تاسیس as a kind of لزوم مالایلزم or one of those
unnecessary things, which an author, by introducing, obliges himself
to continue : thus خاور will rhyme with گوهر—مایل with دل
—تساهل with بلبل

x

The Letters which follow the روي

1. *Wussel* وصل is the letter which immediately follows the روي as ي in the last hemistich of the following distich :

هبچو شبع انکهرا نهاندبهي

در توخندن چوگردنش بزنی

And the letter ه in the following distich :

لا له غافلي تو اي بندہ

دل سیه عبر کو ته و خندہ

The وصل letters most frequently used are ياي مصدري or verbal ي or ياي خطابي or ي indefinite; and ياي تنكري ي and ي in the second person singular; and ميم ضمير متكلم or م of the first person singular; and تاي مخاطب or ت of the second person singular; and شين ضمير غايب or ش in the third person singular; and هاي مضمر آخر كلبه or final ه not sounded, such as هاله and شنيدن and ديدن as ن the verbal نون مصدري and ناله

2. The letter *Kherooj* خروج immediately follows the وصل such as م in the words خوردیم and بردیم and the letter ي as in چیدسي and ديدسي and the letter ت in the words ديدمت and ديدسي

3. *Ma-zeed* مزيد is the letter which immediately follows the خروج such as خوردیهش and بردیهش

4. *Nú-ye-reh* نايره is the letter that immediately follows the مزيد such as ش in the words خورد ستهش and بردستهش and whatever letter follows نايره is accounted belonging to it.

Positions of the Cá-fe-yeh Letters, in relation to the Re-wee.

روي

Following the *Re-wee.*				Preceding the *Re-wee.*			
نايره	مزيد	خروج	وصل	ردف	قيد	تاسيس	دخيل
4	3	2	1	1	2	3	4

The Accents of the Cá-fe-yeh Letters.

The accent over the letter immediately preceding the روي is called *Tow-jeh* توجيه and in the rhymes, any difference between the توجيه is not allowable, excepting when the روي on account of its connection with وصل partakes of its accent, in which case a difference in the accent preceding it is permitted, as in the following distich of Sády :

نيامد درايام او بر دلِي
نگويم که خاري که برگ گلِي

x 2

The accent on the letter preceding ردف and قيد is called
Huz-we حذو The accents of حذو are as follows: when the ردف
is ا then حذو is *Futteh*; upon و is ردف the accent is *Zum*; and
when ي is ردف it is *Kusser*. And قيد has also three variations
of accent, as has been already explained. In the حذو of ردف
no difference is allowable, but it is permitted in قيد provided
روي is accented, as in the following example from Kemál
Ishmáeel:

گر سوز دلم یك نفس آهِسْتَه شود
از دود درون راه نفس بَسْتَه شود
در دیده از ان آب همی گِرد انم
تاهرچه ننقش اوست آن شِسْتَه شود

The *Futteh* preceding تاسیس is called *Rus* رس and the accent
over دخیل is called *Ish-báa* اشباع When the روي is accented,
a difference in the اشباع is allowable, as in the following lines of
Sády:

ای پادشاه وقت چو وقتت فراز شد
تو نیز با گدای محلت برا بِری
مردی گمان مبرکه بسرپنجه است وکتف
با نفس اگر برایی دانم که شاطری

When the روي is joined with the letter وصل it is called *Muj-ré*,
مجري as the *Kussir* of the letter ر in the above verses of Sády:

The accent of the letter وصل when it is joined with خروج is called *Ne-fáz* نغاذ which is the term also given to the accents of خروج and مزيد

Ná-ye-reh نايره is never accented.

Explanation of other Names given to روي and قافيه

When روي is quiescent, it is called *Re-wee Mo-ke-yed* روي مقيد as ن in the words چهن and سخن and when by its union with وصل it obtains an accent, it is called *Re-wee Mut-luk* روي مطلق as ن in چهنم and سخنم and either of these two kinds, if not united with any *Cá-fe-yeh* letter, is called *Mo-jur-rud* مجرد but when it is united with any *Cá-fe-yeh*, it assumes the name thereof. So that روي مقيد مجرد when single, is called روي مقيد and when united with the ردف it is called روي مقيد باردف or *Re-wee*, united with *Ridf*, &c.

The different Kinds of Cá-fe-yeh.

There are four kinds of *Cá-fe-yeh*, viz. 1, *Cá-fe-yeh Mo-jer-rud-eh* قافيه مجرده 2, *Cá-fe-yeh Mo-rud-duf-eh* قافيه مردفه 3, *Cá-fe-yeh Mow-usse-seh* قافيه موسس 4, *Cá-fe-yeh Moo-se eh* قافيه موصله

Of the Defects in Cá-fe-yeh.

1. When روي in one word is quiescent, and in the other is accented, as in the following distich of Háfez,

صلاح كار كجا و من خرابٌ كجا

ببين تفاوت ره از كجا است تا به كجا

this defect is called *Ghoo-loo* غلو If the letter وصل in one word is quiescent, and in the other accented, it is called *Bo-dee* بعدي

2. When the *Tow-jeh* توجيه in the two words are differently accented, it is called *Uk-wá* اقوي which has been exemplified under the head of *Tow-jeh* توجيه

3. A difference in the روي which is an unpardonable error, although some admit it, when the *Re-wee* in one letter has an Arabic and in the other a Persian letter; or when the two letters have a proximate utterance, such as لب and چپ and شك and سك — صباح and سپاه and غياث and لباس

But even this is in general disallowed. This fault is called *Ik-fá* اكفا

4. Disagreement in the ردف which is allowed by Arabic Poets, but in Persian is absolutely inadmissible. The Arabians rhyme حميل with نزول and بدور with منير and such like.

RHYME. 159

5. Disagreement in the letter قيد on account of distance of utterance, such as rhyming عبر and شعر—دزد and درد which however is not very vicious, and has been used by several Poets.

6. Disagreement is the اشباع * when the روي is مقيد such as تجاهل and كامل

7. Disagreement in the حذ such as نور and دور The three last kinds of defects are called *Se-nád* سناد

8. *Ee-ta* ايطا in Arabic, and in Persian *Shá-ye-gon* شايگان is repeating same word in verses in one sense; but when it is repeated with different significations, it is not called *Ee-ta*, being of the nature of *Tuj-nees* تجنيس *Ee-ta* is of two kinds, 1 *Khe-feė*, and 2, *Je-lee*.

1. *Khe-fee* خفي is when the repetition is not striking, such as سرگردان and حيران or بينا and دانا &c.

2. *Je-lee* جلي is when the repetition is apparent, such as فسونكر and ستمگر or حاجتمند and درمند &c. And such as ا and ن occurring together in the words ياران and دوستان and such as ي and ن in the words سيمين and زرين and such as ها in the words كلها and باغها and such as بكرد and نكرد and بكن and مرا and را and مكن

* See page 156, line 14.

6

This second kind of *Ee-ta* is very inelegant, and can never be admitted in the same distich; but after the intervention of some distichs, it may be allowed in a *Ká-see-deh* or *Ghuz-el* or *Ke-tad*.

9. *Tuz-meen* تضمين is when the sense of the rhyme rests upon what is to follow, as in this tetrastich of Ameer Khusro:

در حسن ترا كسئ نهاند الا
خورشيد كه هر صبح برون آيدتا
خدمت كند و پاي تو بوسد اما
نايي تو بسوي او كه تا بوسد پا

10. When the rhyme of a *Ká-see-deh* or *Ke-tad* undergoes a change, and which is a very great deformity, unless the alteration is designed and pointed out, as in a *Ká-see-deh* of Sheikh Azoo-ree, beginning thus:

نماز شام كه از گردش قضا و قدر
زبام چرخ با فتاد خسر و خاور

After some distichs, he then points out the change of the rhyme:

بناي قافيه را يك الف زياده كنم
بشرط انكه نگيرند خورده اهل هنر
سوال كرده ام از نورديده ابزار
كه اي بذات تو آورده كاينات اقرار

11. *Tuk-rár Cá-fe-yeh Má-mool* تكرار قافيه معمول or repetition of the *Má-mool* rhyme. The *Má-mool* rhyme is formed either by separating or by compounding; the latter, as in the following distich of Háfez :

ميكشي و بغمزه ميكوبي
توبه كردي زعشق يانه هنوز

The *Mut-lá* of this *Ghuz-el* is

مبستم ازباده شبانه هنوز
ساقي ما نرفته خانه هنوز

And also in the following tetrastich of the author of this treatise :

كرشمع نه دلجوبي پروانه كند
بر آتش او ز دور پروانه كند
فرياد زشمع من كه درآ تش عشق
پروانه صفت سوزم و پرو انكند

The other kind is when a word is divided into two parts, one of which is made *Cá-fe-yeh* or rhyme, and the other becomes رديف as in the following tetrastichs of Shums eddeen of Delhy, the author of this treatise.

هرقدر او عتاب و نازارد
دل بيچاره ام نياز ارد
به كه آن دلربا برغم رفت
بعد ازين خاطرم نيازارد

Both these kinds, when skilfully managed, are great beauties in poetry; but when repeated, or introduced injudiciously, become deformities.

Of the Distribution of the Cá-fe-yeh, *according to the Measure.*

Khá-leel Ebn Ahmed has limited the *Cá-fe-yeh* to two quiescents, as has already been intimated in the commencement of this treatise; and, according to this rule, *Cá-fe-yeh* cannot exceed four kinds.

1. When the two quiescents occur without any intervention, as in the following distich of Se-nà-ee:

$$نايب مصطفي بروز غدير$$
$$كرده درشرع خود مر اورا مبر ١$$

This kind of *Cá-fe-yeh,* is called *Mo-ta-rá-dif* مترادف

2. When the two quiescents are separated by an accented letter, thus:

$$درصف رزم پاي او محكم$$
$$و زيب امر جان او محرم$$

This kind is called *Mo-ta-wá-tir,* متواتر

6

3. When two accented letters occur between the two quiescents, as in the following distich of Khá-cánee:

جوشن صورت برون کن در صف مردان دراي
دل طلب کز دارملک دل توان شد پا'د'شا

The letter د in پادشا in scanning is accented. This kind of Cá-fe-yeh is called Mo-te-dá-rek متدارک

4. When three accented letters intervene between the two quiescents, as in the following distich of Se-ná-ee:

نور اوبت شکن زرو زازل
دست او تیغ زن براوج زحل

This kind of Cá-fe-yeh is called Mo-te-rá-keb متراکب

Mo-te-ká-wus متکاوس is when four accented letters intervene between the two quiescents, which is common in Arabic, but not allowable in Persian poetry.

Of Re-deef ردیف

Re-deef signifies an independent word or words which are introduced at the end of hemistichs or distichs after the rhyme is completed, as in the following distich of Ze-hoo-ree:

درآه و ناله تقصیری نکردم
چه حاصل فکر تاثیری نکردم

According to Nás-seer-ed-deen Tou-see, the *Re-deef* is a repeti-
tition of the word without any variation of the sense; but it may
be used throughout a *Ká-see-deh,* either with one, or with various
significations.

All, excepting Nás-seer-ed-deen, agree that the *Re-deef* ought to
have a signification in itself, independent of the rhyme.   And it is
allowable for the hemistich to be composed solely of the *Cá-fe-yeh*
and the *Re-deef,* as in the following tetrastich of Jami :

من درغم هجر و دل بدید ار تو خوش
تن درغم هجر و دل بدید ار تو خوش
تا کی چشم سرشک حسرت ریزد
اندرغم هجر و دل بدید ار تو خوش

Any change in the *Re-deef* is not allowable, unless the intended
alteration is pointed out, as in a *Ká-see-deh* of Kemál Is-máeel,
beginning thus :

سپیده دم که نسیم بهار می آمد
نگاه کردم و دیدم که یار می آمد

After some distichs in the *Ká-see-deh,* he thus points out an alteration of the *Re-deef.*

زیهر فال زماضي شدم بهستقبل
که برا نام چنین خوشگوارمي آید

Há-jeb حاجب is that kind of *Re-deef* which is introduced between two rhymes.

INDEX OF TERMS EXPLAINED

IN

THIS WORK.

THE END.

PRINTED BY WILSON & CO.
ORIENTAL PRESS,

EAST INDIA PUBLICATIONS,

PRINTED FOR

J. DEBRETT, *oppofite Burlington Houfe, Piccadilly.*

THE ASIATIC ANNUAL REGISTER; or, A VIEW of the HISTORY of HINDUSTAN, and of the Politics, Commerce, and Literature of Asia, for the Year 1800. To which is prefixed, a Continuation of the History of India, comprehending a View of the Commercial Intercourse between that Country and Europe, of the Rife and Progrefs of the Portuguefe Trade and Eftablifhments in the Eaft, and of the Caufes of their Declenfion and Fall. In one large volume 8vo. Price 13s. in boards.

The ASIATIC ANNUAL REGISTER for 1799: to which is prefixed a Hiftory of India, from the earlieft ages to 1603. The Second Edition, correóted.

The NEW EAST INDIA KALENDAR for 1801: containing complete and accurate Lifts of all the Civil, and Military Eftablifhments of the Honourable Eaft India Company, at their feveral Prefidencies and Faótories in the Eaft Indies, China, and the Ifland of St. Helena. Alfo, General Lifts of the Civil Servants, of the different Corps of the Armies at the refpeótive Settlements, and of European Settlements in India; with feparate Indexes to each Department. To which is prefixed, a List of the Company's Eftablifhment at Home, compiled from the Original Documents at the India Houfe. By ROBERT HUDSON, of the Office of Examiner of India Correfpondence. Illuftrated by a correót Map of India.

A LETTER from the Right Hon. HENRY DUNDAS, to the Chairman, Deputy Chairman, and Court of Direótors of the Eaft India Company, June 20, 1801; with an Appendix of Official Papers. Price 5s.

The PERSIAN MOONSHEE; containing the Grammatical Rules, the Pund Namch of Sadi, Forms of Addrefs, Seleót Tales and Pleafing Stories, Lives of the Philofophers, Kowayed us Sultanet Shah-Jehan, Dialogues, and fome Chapters of the Gofpel of St. Matthew, with Notes by the late William Chambers, Esq. all in Perfian, with Englifh Tranflations. By FRANCIS GLADWIN, Efq. of Calcutta. In one volume royal quarto, hotpreffed, elegantly printed in the new Talik Type caft by Figgins for Wilfon and Co. of the Oriental Prefs, and illuftrated with 32 Plates, containing exaót Imitations of Perfian and Arabic Manufcripts. Price 3l. 3s. in boards. ☞ This Work will be found to contain every requifite inftruótion for thofe who may wifh to obtain a thorough knowledge of the Perfian Language, and to render the moft difficult hand-writing perfeótly familiar.

The BAKHTYAR NAMEH, or Story of Prince Bakhtyar and the Ten Viziers, a Series of Perfian Tales; from a Manufcript in the Colleótion of Sir WILLIAM OUSELEY. Perfian and Englifh. Elegantly printed in royal 8vo. Price 14s. in boards. ☞ A few Copies of the Englifh Tranflation may be had feparate.

The TOOTI NAMEH, or Tales of the Parrot; in the Perfian Language, with an Englifh Tranflation. Elegantly printed in royal 8vo. hot-preffed, the Perfian Types by Vincent Figgins. Price 18s. in boards. ☞ Of this Work it would be almoft a fufficient recommendation to obferve, that it is one of the valuable and numerous Publications of the celebrated Mr. GLADWIN, and that this Edition has been undertaken in confequence of the impoffibility of procuring a copy of the original in this country, and the difficulty and delay in getting one from Calcutta. It will be found equally entertaining to the General Reader, as interefting to the Orientalift, and peculiarly inftruótive to the Student of the Perfian Language. The fubjeót turns principally on Gallantry, the plots are managed with ingenuity, and the narrative related with delicacy; and the whole affords a very curious pióture of Afiatic manners.

The PRINCIPLES of ASIATIC MONARCHIES, Politically and Hiftorically inveftigated, and contrafted with thofe of the Monarchies of Europe; fhewing the dangerous tendency of confounding them in the Adminiftration of the Affairs of India. With an attempt to trace this Difference to its fource. By ROBERT PATTON, Efq. Governor of the Ifland of St. Helena, and Author of an Hiftorical Review of the Monarchy and Republic of Rome, 8vo.

A DICTIONARY, ENGLISH, PERSIAN, and ARABIC. By JOHN RICHARDSON, Efq. M.A. F.S.A. of the Middle Temple, and of Wadham College, Oxford. In 2 vols. folio. Price 16l. 16s. bound.

PERSIAN LYRICS, or Scattered Poems from the Diwan-I-Hafiz; with Paraphrafes, in Verfe and Profe; a Catalogue of the Gazels, as arranged in a Manufcript of the Works of Hafiz in the Chetham Library at Manchefter, and other Illuftrations. By the Rev. Mr. HINDLEY.